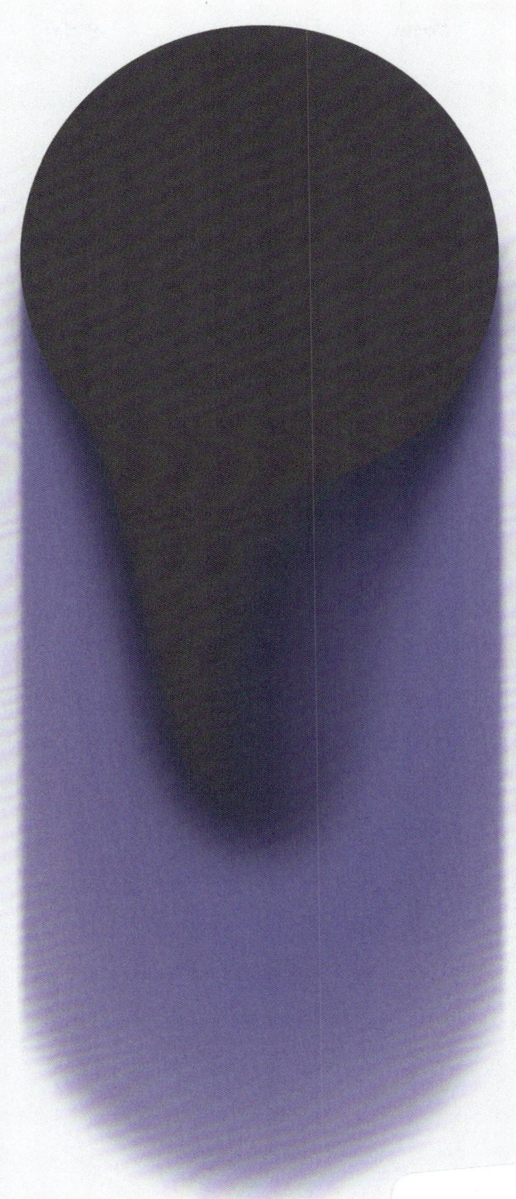

AF478865

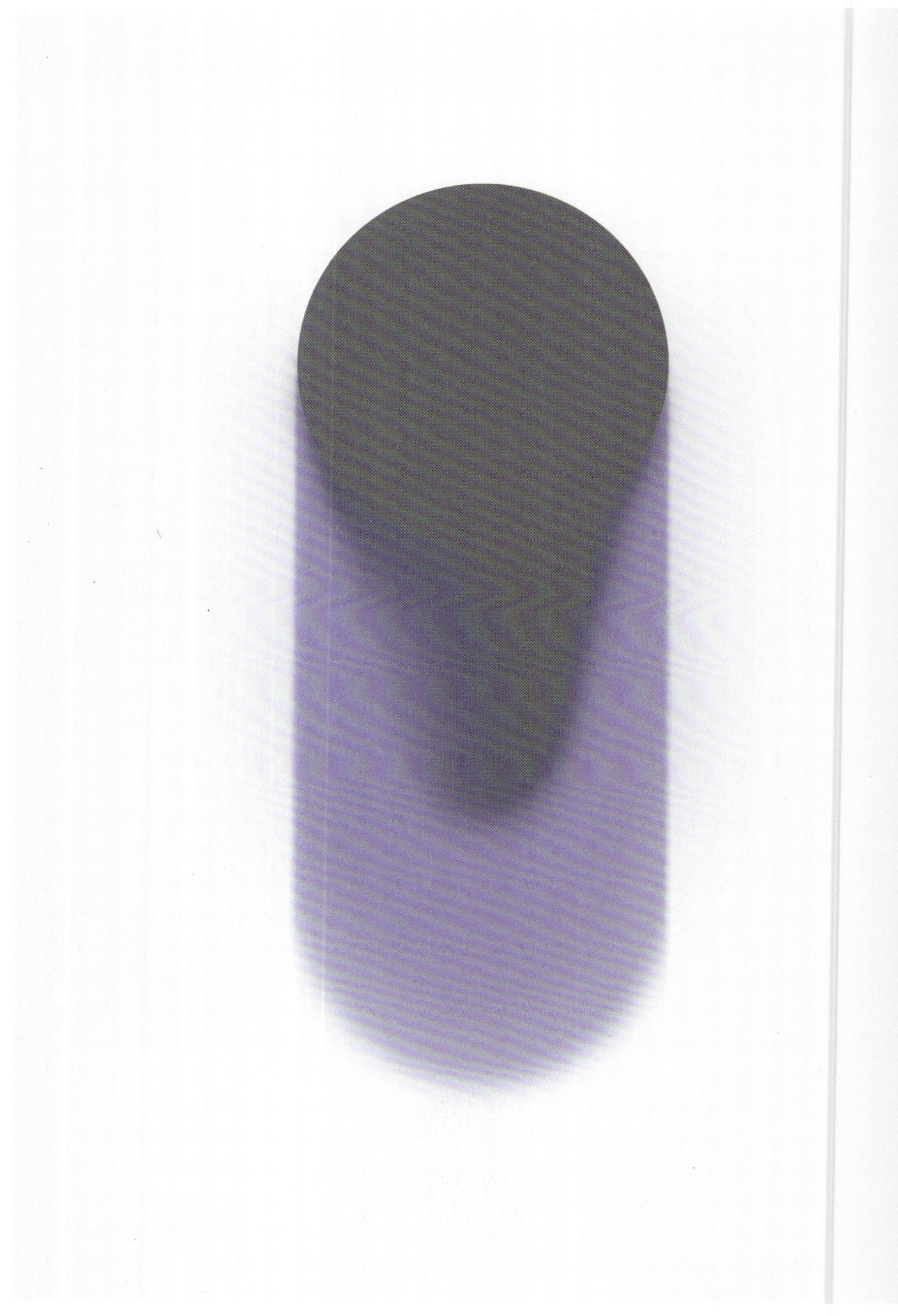

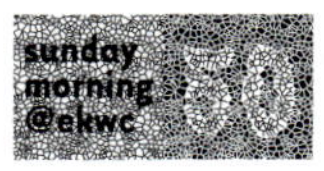
nai
010
sunday
morning
@ekwc
50
DESIGN
MUSEUM
DEN
BOSCH

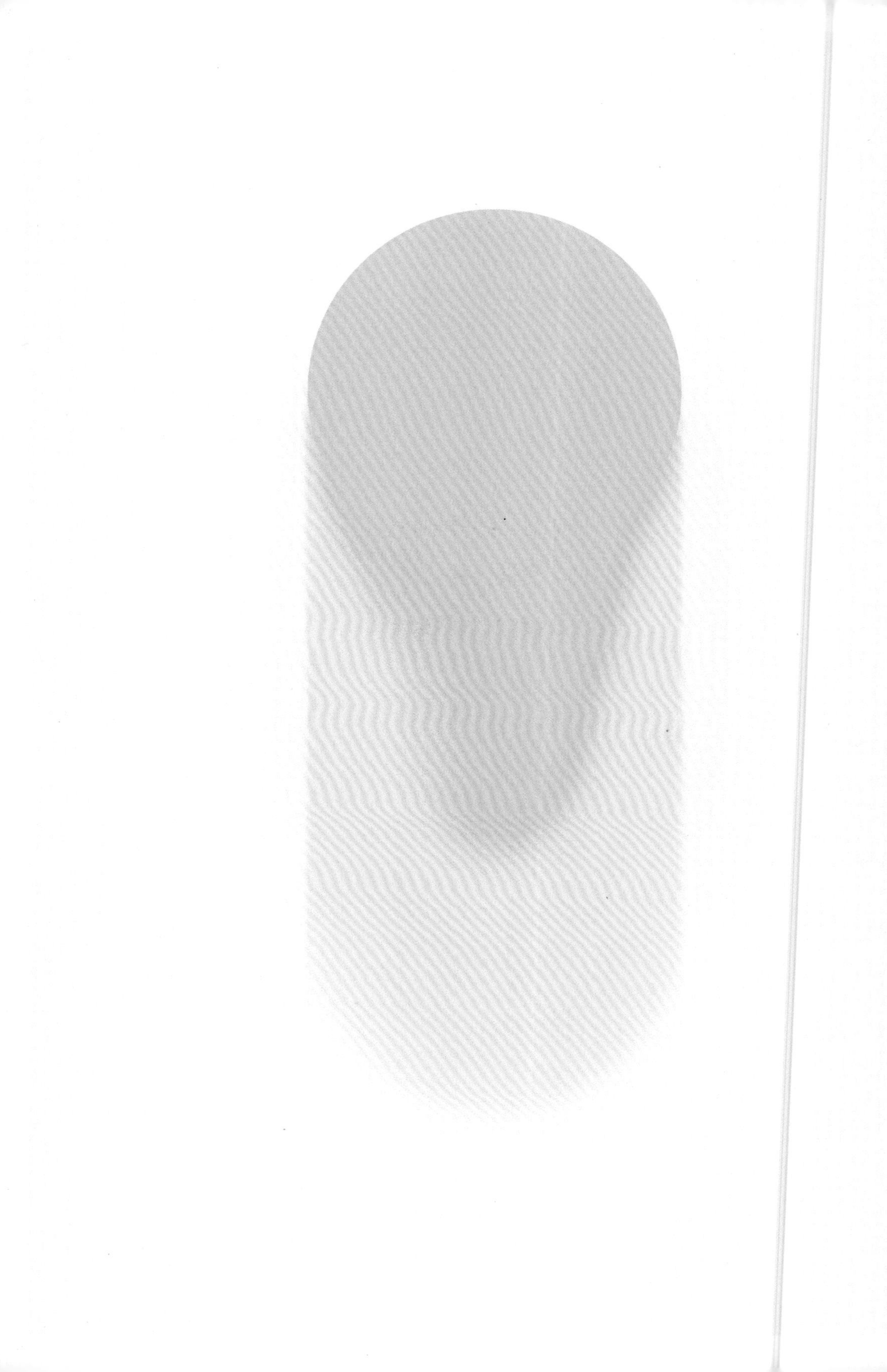

The Ghosts
of Sunday
Morning

Contents

The Ghosts of Sunday Morning

The European Ceramic Work Centre (EKWC) and Design Museum Den Bosch are from the same generation and have a long shared history. Both institutions have led a somewhat restless existence. The EKWC was founded in 1969 and was renamed Sundaymorning@EKWC in 2011. The forerunner to our museum existed at the time as a study collection of ceramics and was housed in an official museum 15 years later. The EKWC began in Heusden, was long based in Den Bosch and made a new start, after winning a battle for funding, in a beautiful location in Oisterwijk.

by
Timo de Rijk

The Design Museum was first called Museum het Kruithuis and housed in the seventeenth-century military building of the same name, after which, following several temporary accommodations, it found a home in the present new-build premises in the Museum Quarter.

availability and his willingness were still up in the air. Adamson is the world's most important craft curator, and he immediately agreed. He made his name with trendsetting publications on craft, and following appointments at the V&A Museum in London and the Museum of Arts and Design in New York, he has become a curator of international authority who produces exhibitions and gives lectures all over the world.

We were even more enthusiastic when Glenn presented his plan for 'The Ghosts of Sunday Morning'. The central idea of the exhibition and this publication is to recreate, at scale, a selection of works from 50 years of EKWC history. The final objects are not historical remnants; instead they function as reflections of this history. In an unexpected and ingenious way, the project plays with the question of what an original object is, which story the object tells in a museum and what the relationship between a place of making and a museum exhibition hall is. Initially, however, all of this existed only on paper. It is thanks to the incredible skill and effort of the people at the EKWC that the objects for this exhibition, the Ghosts, could actually be produced.

To make this project possible, highly appreciated contributions came from the North Brabant Prince Bernhard Culture Fund and the Creative Industries Fund NL, for which I wish to express my heartfelt thanks. I am also keen to thank, on behalf of Ranti Tjan and the entire EKWC as well, Glenn Adamson for his dedication and beautiful ideas. And finally, on behalf of the museum, I wish to congratulate the European Ceramic Work Centre on its anniversary.

Timo de Rijk
Director, Design Museum Den Bosch

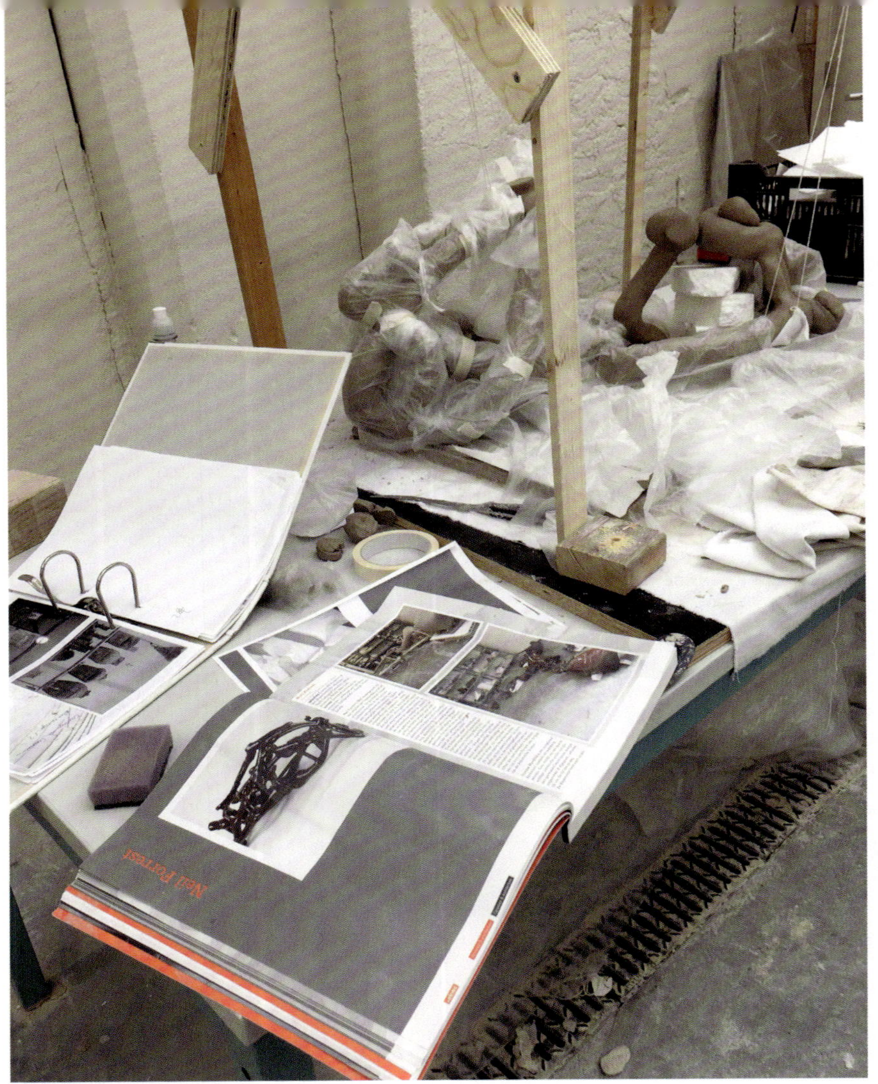

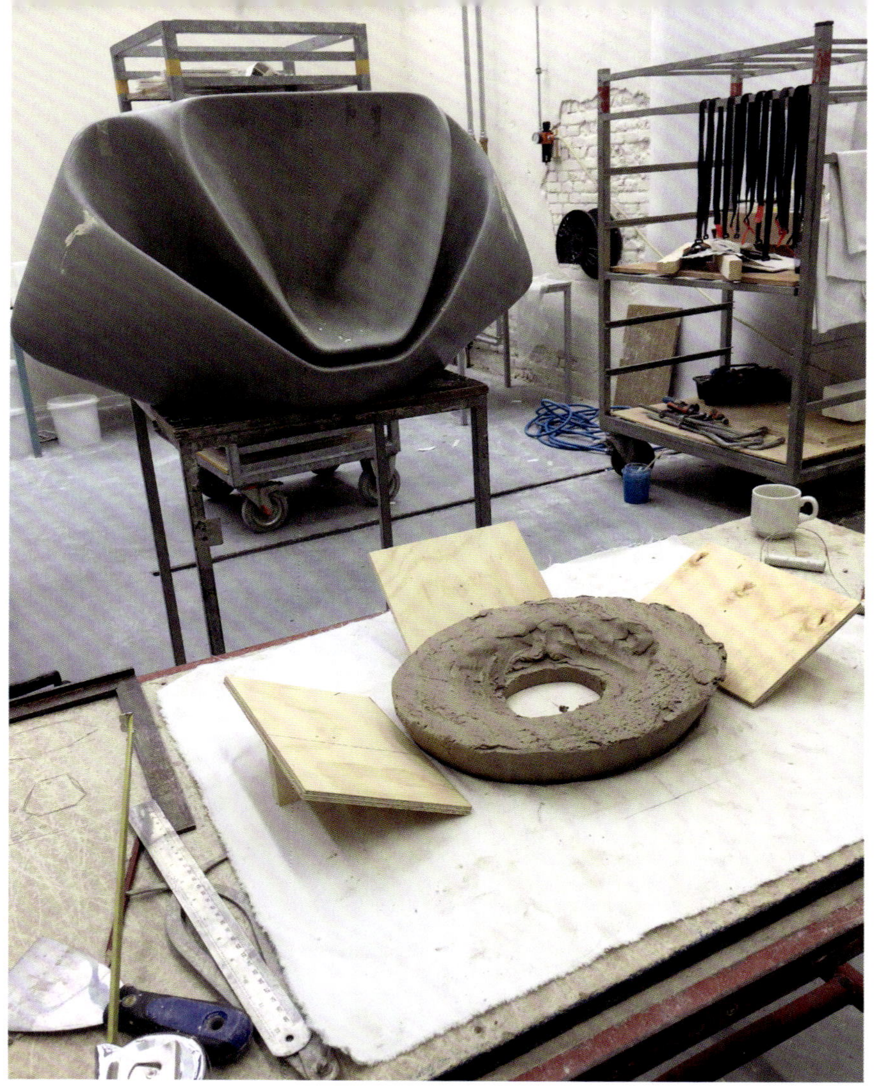

The Ghosts of Sunday Morning

When an artist submits an application for residency at the European Ceramic Work Centre, the first people to evaluate it are the advisors. This is a team of skilled makers, currently six in number: Sander Alblas, Froukje van Baren, Katrin König, Peter Oltheten, Marianne Peijnenburg and Pierluigi Pompei. They carefully review the submissions, setting to one side the projects that seem wildly improbable, hard to understand or impossible to realize. They mark this pile: *highest priority for acceptance.*

by
Glenn Adamson

The advisors' role in the Centre – recently rebranded as Sundaymorning@EKWC – is not easy to summarize. But over the five decades of the institution's history they have been the continuous link. Initially a modestly scaled communal workshop located in the town of Heusden, the organization moved to Den Bosch in 1991, and in 2015 to its present site in Oisterwijk. At these three different facilities, the Centre has served more than 1,400 artists. The advisors are in many ways the heart and soul of the operation. Their primary role is to provide advice, but they may also lend a hand in the making of the work, assisting as necessary in the processes of making, drying, glazing and firing, preparing a mould, or managing digital rendering and fabrication. They also assist resident artists in informal ways, helping to connect them to resources locally or further afield in the Netherlands, or simply offering moral support. One thing they are not is fabricators, who simply receive a design and execute it, no questions asked. Nor do they share in the authorship of the works made at Sundaymorning@EKWC – they're quite clear on this point – not even in a collaborative sense. The role of the advisors is at once essential and circumspect, totally hands-on, but done with the lightest of touch. The Centre has world-class equipment, a high calibre and wide range of participant artists and, by this point, an international stature in its own right, which adds lustre to any project undertaken there. But when people say that this place is a kind of creative paradise, it's really the advisors they have in mind.

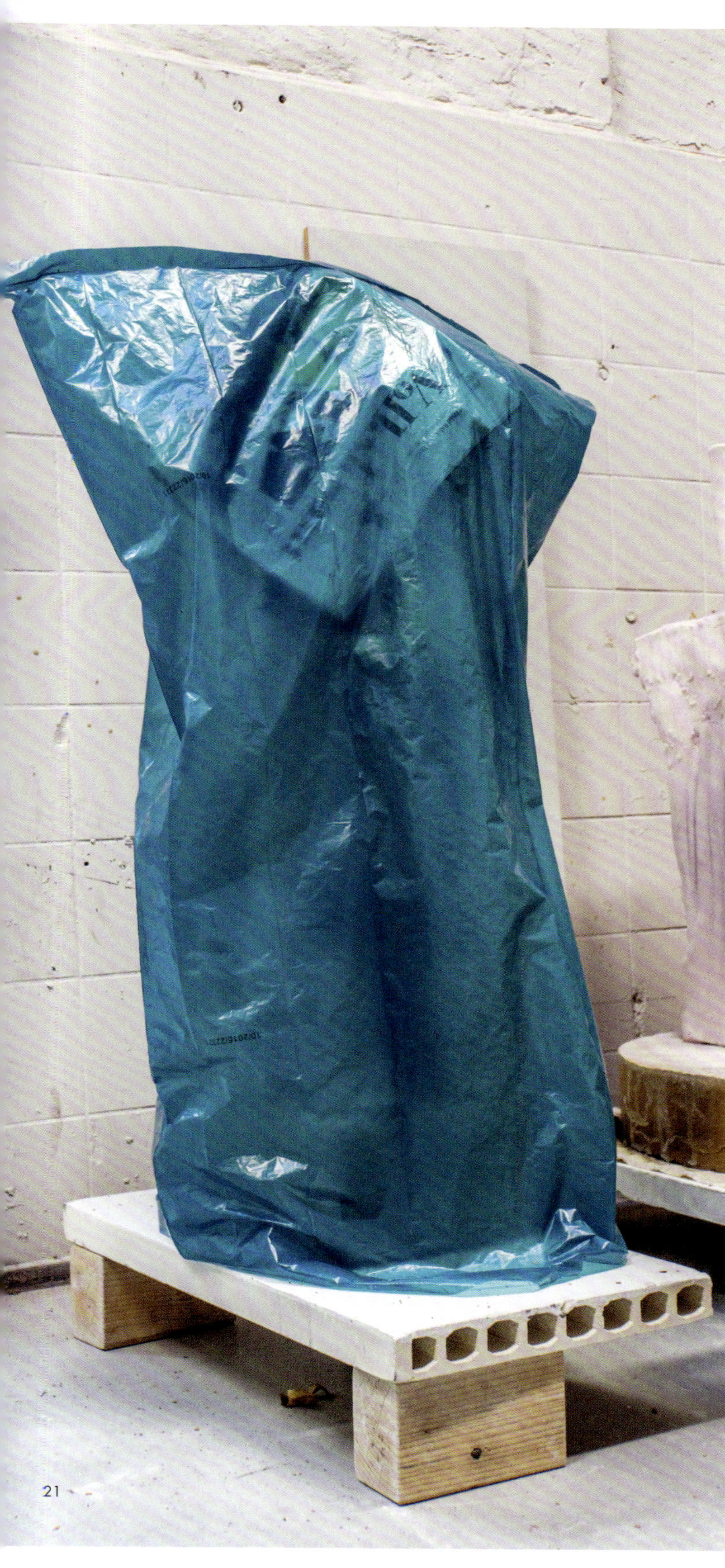

When I was approached to curate an exhibition on
the occasion of Sundaymorning@EKWC's fiftieth
anniversary, I knew immediately that I wanted to tell the
advisors' story. One of the most striking things about the
organization is its democratic spirit; every artist is treated
the same, with identical opportunities and identical
expectations (they take turns making dinner, for example,
the only aspect of the residency that gets competitive).
Previously though, as pretty much everywhere in the art
world, a hierarchy has been observed. Attention and
publicity has been reserved mainly for participating
artists, with the advisors operating behind the scenes.
Recently, there has been a tendency in contemporary
art to be more transparent about production models,
including the crediting of various types of fabricators. I
wanted our show to be part of that new way of thinking,
and even to chart new ground. Rarely if ever has an art
museum exhibition showcased the skills and perspective
of the technical staff. That is what I wanted to do.

The question was how. Like other artisans working in
the art field, the advisors are typically uncredited even
in cases where they have been heavily involved. This
in itself would make it difficult to create an
exhibition about past advisors at the Centre
– of whom there have been many (during
the organization's years at Den Bosch, when
it received more government funding, there
were sometimes 20 or more on staff). Even
if we could somehow reconstruct which
advisors had helped out with various projects
at Sundaymorning@EKWC over the years, no
matter how carefully selected, the exhibition
might feel a bit random – individual works
by artists very different from one another,
without any coherent aesthetic theme.

Eventually, I proposed an idea to Ranti Tjan,
the imaginative and innovative director of
the Centre, and to Timo de Rijk, the equally

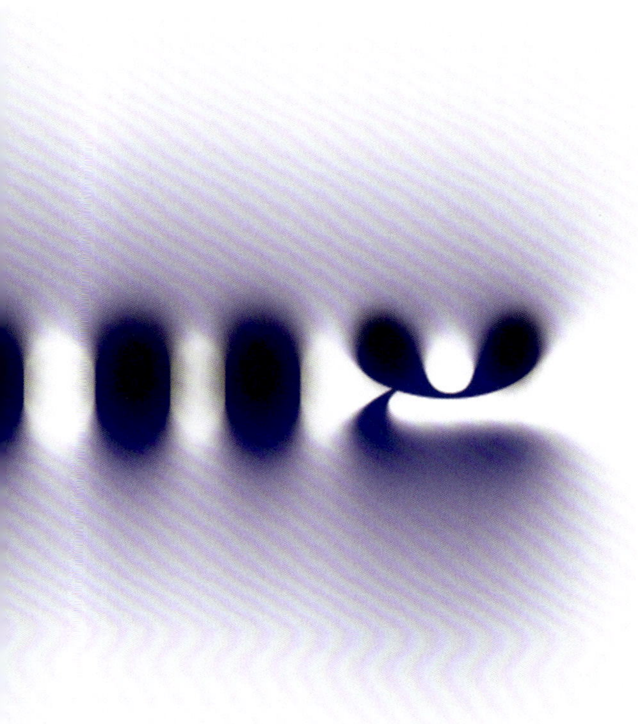

enterprising director of the Design Museum Den Bosch.
The Centre's greatest asset has always been its own
extraordinary productive capabilities: Why not ask the
current staff to *remake* past works? This would allow us
to represent the achievements of Sundaymorning@EKWC
while putting the spotlight on the advisors, right where I
wanted it.

They agreed. With some assistance from a team of
supporting technicians and interns, the six advisors
would be asked to recreate more than 30 works, each
one the original conception of a past artist resident.
But these would not be literal copies. That would be
impossible, in purely practical terms. In many cases,
we would not have the original work of art to refer to,
and the advisors would instead have to base their own
creation on a single photo, perhaps inferring its overall
three-dimensional shape from an image showing only
one side. In any case, none of us wanted to mimetically
reproduce an artist's work. That would trespass to a
degree on their authorship, precisely the conclusion that
Sundaymorning@EKWC aims to avoid at all costs. The
advisors' recreations would be new things in the world,
portraits of past works, not duplicates.

As the conversation proceeded, we decided to further
emphasize this quality of interpretive transformation by
adopting two rules. First, the recreations would all be
made in a single material: white stoneware clay. This
would lend the display a visual coherence, and equally
importantly, would convey the idea that these objects
had only partially returned from the past. We began
calling them 'ghosts'. This approach seemed appropriate
not only to the occasion of an anniversary, but also to
the character of the medium. Fired ceramics have a
somewhat haunted quality, in the way that they preserve
for all time quick and incidental occurrences – a maker's
fingerprints, the inscribed line of a tool, the slump of the
clay itself.

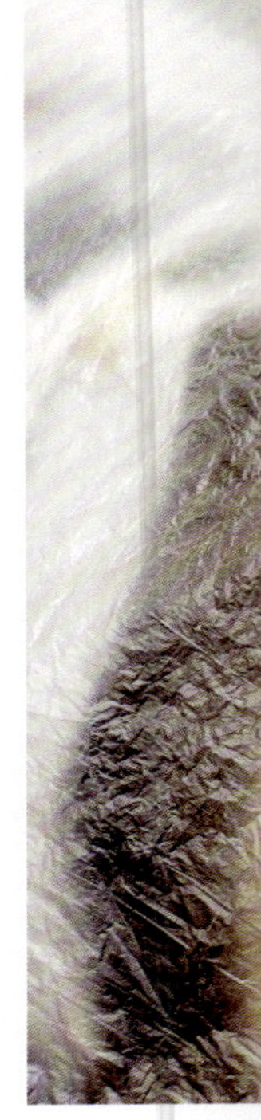

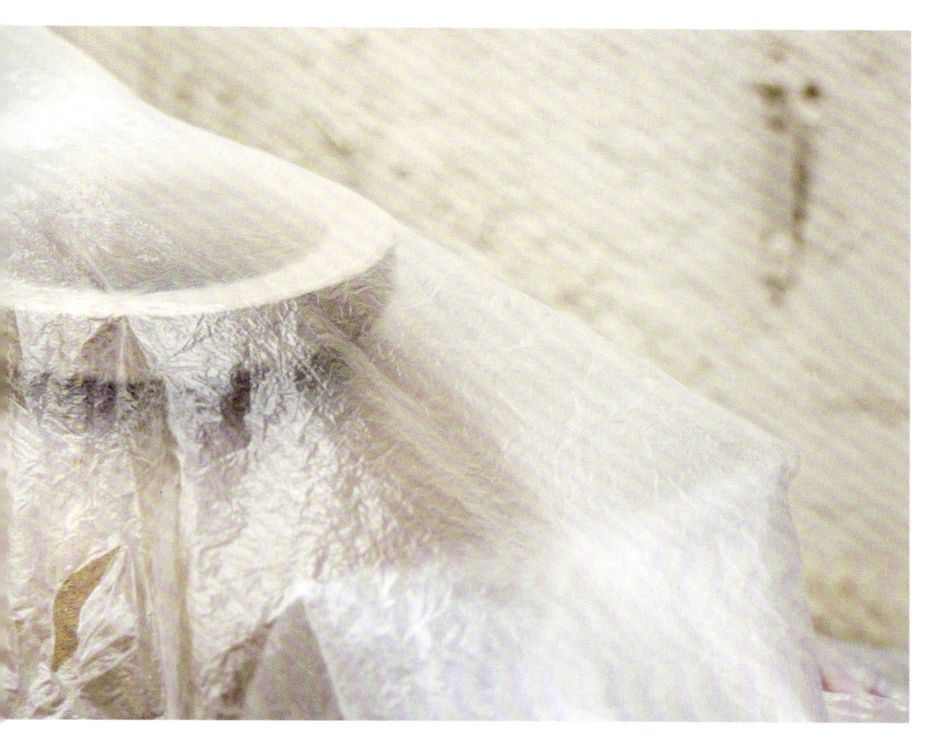

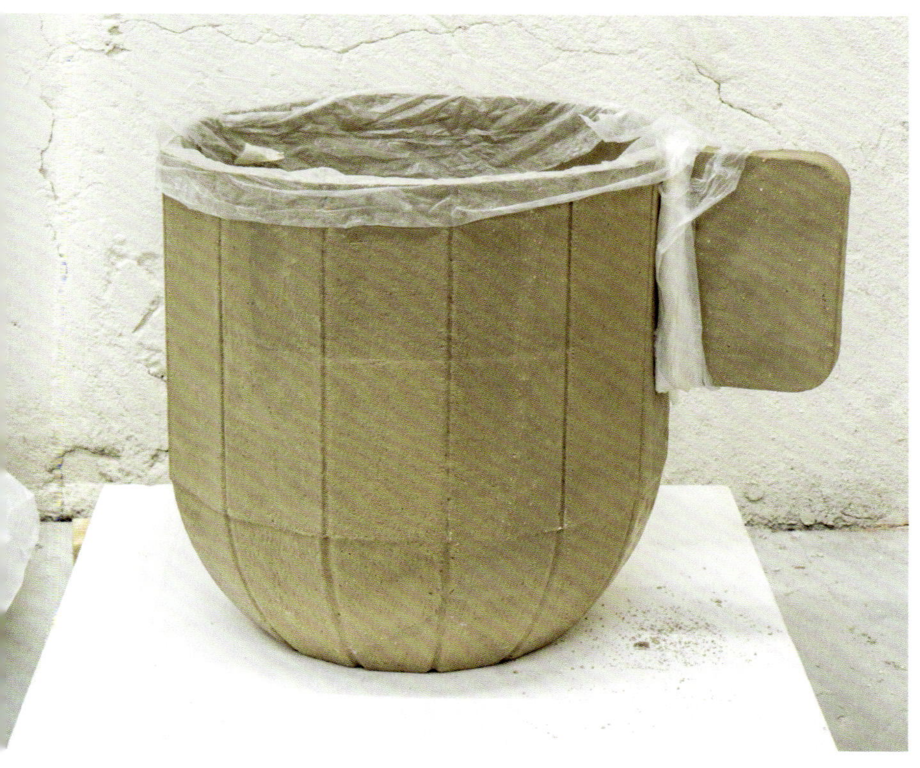

The second rule had to do with scale. We were presented with a dilemma: the works to be re-created were highly various in size. Some were very large. In some cases, we did not have precise dimensions. So how big should these 'ghosts' be? The advisors themselves came up with a brilliant solution: they would use exactly the same amount of clay, 50 pounds before drying and firing, to make each work. Though this regulated the task, it also introduced a fascinating wildcard. Objects made of solid clay would of course be smaller than ones that are hollow-cast. A small functional object, like a cup or a piece of jewellery, would become gargantuan; monumental sculptures would be reduced to table-top size. This solution also placed great emphasis on materiality, a principle subject of the show. The consistency in terms of quantity gave the project another interesting angle: it would be a physical demonstration of the myriad things one can accomplish with a given amount of clay.

With the two guidelines in place, the advisors set to work, displaying their customary energy and hyper-competency. They subjected the stoneware clay to a huge diversity of processes: wheel throwing, sculpting, mould making and casting, coiling, slab building, 3D printing, CNC carving. When each piece was completed, the white coat was applied, sheathing its surface particularities, making it a recognizable member of our spectral family. Then it was fired, rendering it – what? A sculpture of a sculpture? A reverse prototype? A miniature monument? A large-scale souvenir? It's hard to say. Together, however they would constitute a memory-tour of Sundaymorning@ EKWC's history: a show of absences, made present.

As a curator, I am delighted by the strangeness of these objects. Their status is unclear, as is their authorship, which seems to be shared by the original artists, the advisors and perhaps myself – putting me in the unusual position of a curator who has (perhaps inadvertently) behaved, just this once, like a conceptual artist. Perhaps this is the

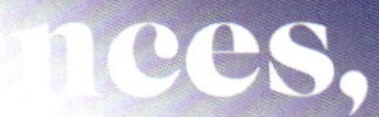

sort of response that Sundaymorning@EKWC brings out in people. Come into contact with the place, and your sense of the possible enlarges, to the point where it starts to feel crazy *not* to take a risk.

The process of making the ghosts involves transformation on several registers. There is of course the original premise: the interpretive reinvention of an existing work of art. Each of the recreations is recognizably based on its original, but the differences are sometimes quite extreme, as great as the difference between a map and a territory. Then there is an associated shift in the advisors' work. Typically their role involves an imaginative projection of what might be, in the near future. They work closely with the resident artists, who may arrive with only an indeterminate idea of what they want to achieve. Even in cases where participants do have an extremely detailed plan, there are inevitably surprises, swerves along the creative pathway. These may come about for technical reasons, or simply because of a realization of new avenues of exploration. In this project, by contrast, the advisors began from an endpoint and worked backward: an already established form, by virtue of the blankness and approximation of the ghosting process, would be devolved into a vaguer condition.

Like anything remembered, the ghosts are less definite than a primary experience. They summon a sense of distance. Indeed, the way that they have grown or diminished in scale seems a nice metaphor for the workings of psychology. For reasons that may well be hard to understand, certain past events or objects may dwell in the mind even though they initially seemed unimportant, attaining an outsized presence in our awareness. Conversely, an encounter that once seemed foundational may, in retrospect, shrink into a minor role in the narrative of the self.

In the making of our phantom objects, there was also, of course, a more fundamental transformation: the transmutation of raw clay into form. This is the bedrock reality of the discipline, and of Sundaymorning@EKWC. And boy oh boy, is it hard to master. Even given the most consistent clays, the best equipment, and the highest levels of skill, all of which exist at the Centre, ceramics are constantly surprising, and not necessarily in a good way. At the point when the work has been formed, its journey is just beginning. First it must be

allowed to dry, typically wrapped in plastic
sheeting to control the rate of water loss. This
stage requires constant vigilance, as uneven
moisture levels or too-rapid evaporation
can produce cracking. Kiln firing too, is a
legendarily risky stage. If things go spectacu-
larly wrong, there is the potential to suddenly
lose weeks or months of preparation in a
matter of hours. Even if all goes to plan, clay
contracts in the kiln; usually by about 4 per
cent while drying and by 6 per cent in the
oven, so 10 per cent in total. This is a totally
predictable effect but nonetheless catches
most people new to the medium off-guard.
Without experience it's quite difficult to understand what that amount of shrinkage will
really look like. (For painters working with
ceramics, there is a comparable learning
curve in managing glaze colours, which look
completely different before and after firing.)

The advisors know their business as well as
anyone, and better than most. But like all
experienced ceramists, they know how to
cope with occasional disappointment. All
the more so as Sundaymorning@EKWC is
famous for pushing the possibilities of the
discipline right to the limit. They are adven-
turous not only at application stage, but
throughout the whole of the process. In fact,
advisors will sometimes purposefully suggest
uncharted technical options to a resident.
This is not because they love courting risk
(indeed, much of their skill is in minimizing
it), but because that's where innovation is
most likely to occur. Each resident, no matter
what the level of their previous exposure
to clay, is guaranteed to have an intensive
learning experience while at the Centre, and
the staff learns right along with them. Over

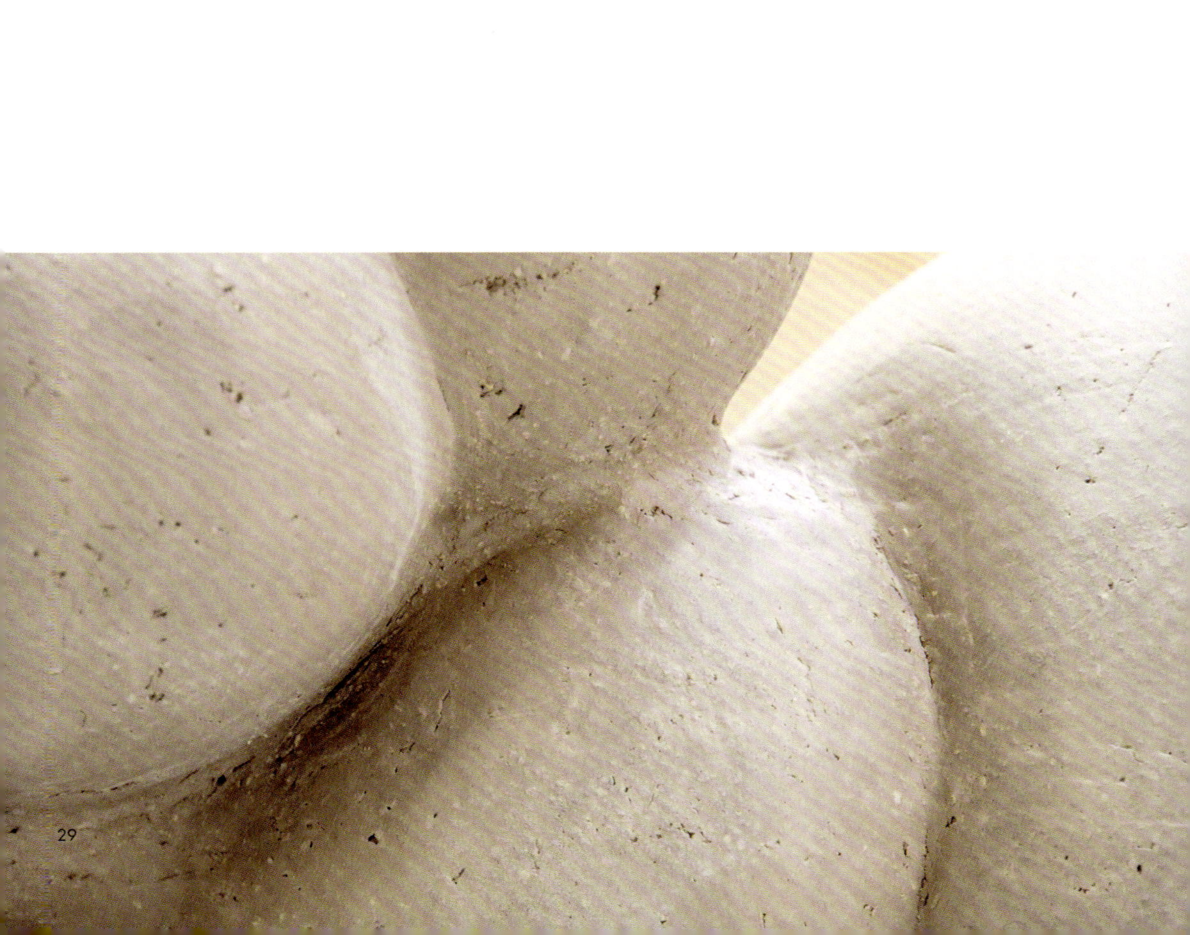

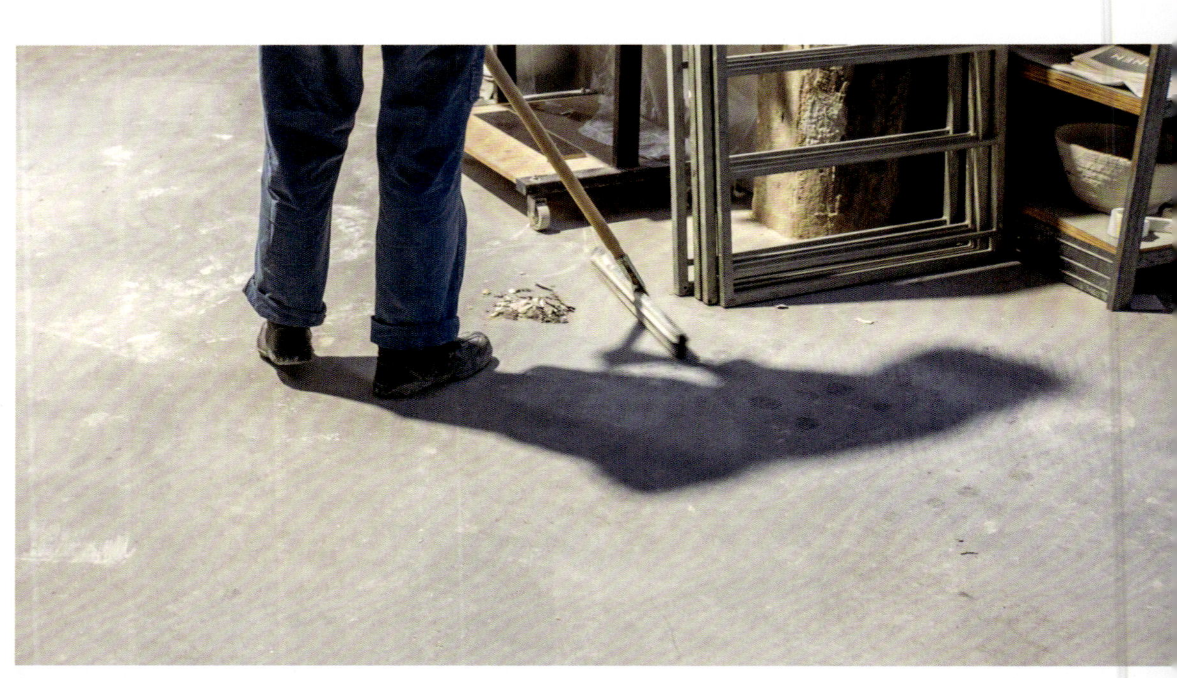

the years this has made for an extraordinary repository
of accumulated knowledge. It never stops. By raising the
stakes on one project after another, the advisors expand
their own horizons, and those of the artists that come to
work with them.

Having set the parameters for our unusual show, the next
step was to select the works to be ghosted. This afore-
mentioned unpredictability of ceramics was one of the
themes I had in mind, hence my choices of Tim Breukers'
Big Bag (2011) – which finds its expression in the way
that buckling clay establishes its own contours, in silent
partnership with the maker – as well as the sublimely
irregular *Thicket* (2005) by Neil Forrest, and a sculpture
by eminent British sculptor Anish Kapoor, in which a
perfect geometrical dome appears to emerge from (or
possibly sink into) a rifted clod.

There was a lot else to choose from, too. Over the course
of its 50 years, and particularly once the Centre shifted
its activities primarily to working with fine artists – many
of whom had no experience with clay prior to their residency – the output of Sundaymorning@EKWC has been
extraordinarily various. It ranges from giant sculptures
to building tiles, from functional pots to conceptual art.
When I last visited, there were sculptors and potters on
residency, but also a jeweller and a sound artist. The
place is truly a crossroads of art, craft and design
(and a reminder that those categories are forever
colliding and overlapping with one another). My checklist
reflected this, with works originating in disciplines of
architecture and product design as well as abstract and
figurative fine art.

Given the ventriloquistic methods of the exhibition, there
was also an opportunity to consider another aspect of
ceramics, which is perhaps underappreciated by the
general public. Much of the discourse surrounding clay
is, understandably, rooted in tactile experience. Many
people have their very first experiences of making with

clay, as young children. Even adults can
appreciate its cool squelch in the palm
and, equally, the way that a finished and
functional ceramic vessel sits warmly in the
hand. Yet only some of the disciplinary skill
set is actually so immediate. Most industrial
ceramics are slip-cast, using prepared
moulds in plaster. These are also among
the most important processes employed at
Sundaymorning@EKWC, allowing for the
translation of an original model into a final
form, often through several discrete steps.
So I wanted to choose works that poetically
expressed this indirect or mediated making.
Among the ghosts speaking most powerfully
to this theme are Stephanie Davison and
Katie Ewald's tiles, and Canan Dagdalen's
untitled work (2011) on the theme of prayer
to Mecca.

In both cases, the original execution
involved the impression of the artist's own
body parts into the clay. Thus these works
already addressed the theme of absence that
is central to our project; they were ghosts
even before we returned to them. When
making their recreations, the Centre's team
had to substitute their bodies for those of
the artists, an apt metaphor for the project
as a whole. There is also here, perhaps, a
tacit reflection on the professional role of
the fabricator, who is sometimes treated as
a human tool in the realization of another's
vision. (At an extreme, one thinks here of
Yves Klein's notorious use of naked women
as 'living paintbrushes'.) In our case, though,
the advisors necessarily took control of the
process. They were the ones to determine
who would impress themselves into the clay,
and how. This quasi-repetition of the original

bodily trace, like the exhibition as a whole, suggests not so much a challenge to authorship as a refraction of it, a palpable echo of artistic intention.

Other ghosts occasioned acts of interpretation among the advisors in ways I had not at all predicted. As mentioned above, it was sometimes necessary to interpolate from a single flat image to a complex sculptural form. This was the case with Harumi Nakashima's *Struggling Figure,* a bulbous abstraction of conjoined spheres. It was originally covered with a pattern of blue dots, which are of course lost in the ghost version (an eerie effect also seen in our incarnation of Jun Kaneko's *Italian Dream* from 1996). This much I had anticipated; what was more surprising was the advisors' decision to intentionally change the form of the sculpture, adding two more spheres than in the original, which seemed to them necessary to give it the right sort of balance. At the other end of the spectrum, it turned out that a few of the works I chose for ghosting had originally been produced using digital tools. This meant that a virtual model was still available in the Centre's computer archive, and could be readily reprinted, albeit at a different scale. There's an accidental but satisfying mirroring, here, of another feature of memory: objects less distant in time can quite literally be recalled with greater precision, while those from long ago remain more approximate.

In re-creating other works for the show, the shift in scale required a total shift in process, which in turn resulted in an interesting shift of affect. Andrew Burton's untitled sculpture (2006) composed of small imitation bricks, miniaturized down to 50 pounds, was instead formed in the solid and then inscribed; this doubles down on the *trompe l'oeil* quality of the original. The sculpture *In Camera* (1992), by the great Tony Cragg, is an enor-mous work of ceramic engineering, suggestive of deep-sea bathyspheres. Our ghost version is much smaller, and primarily wheel-thrown. It seems to relate more to vessels for the table than vessels plunging to the ocean floor.

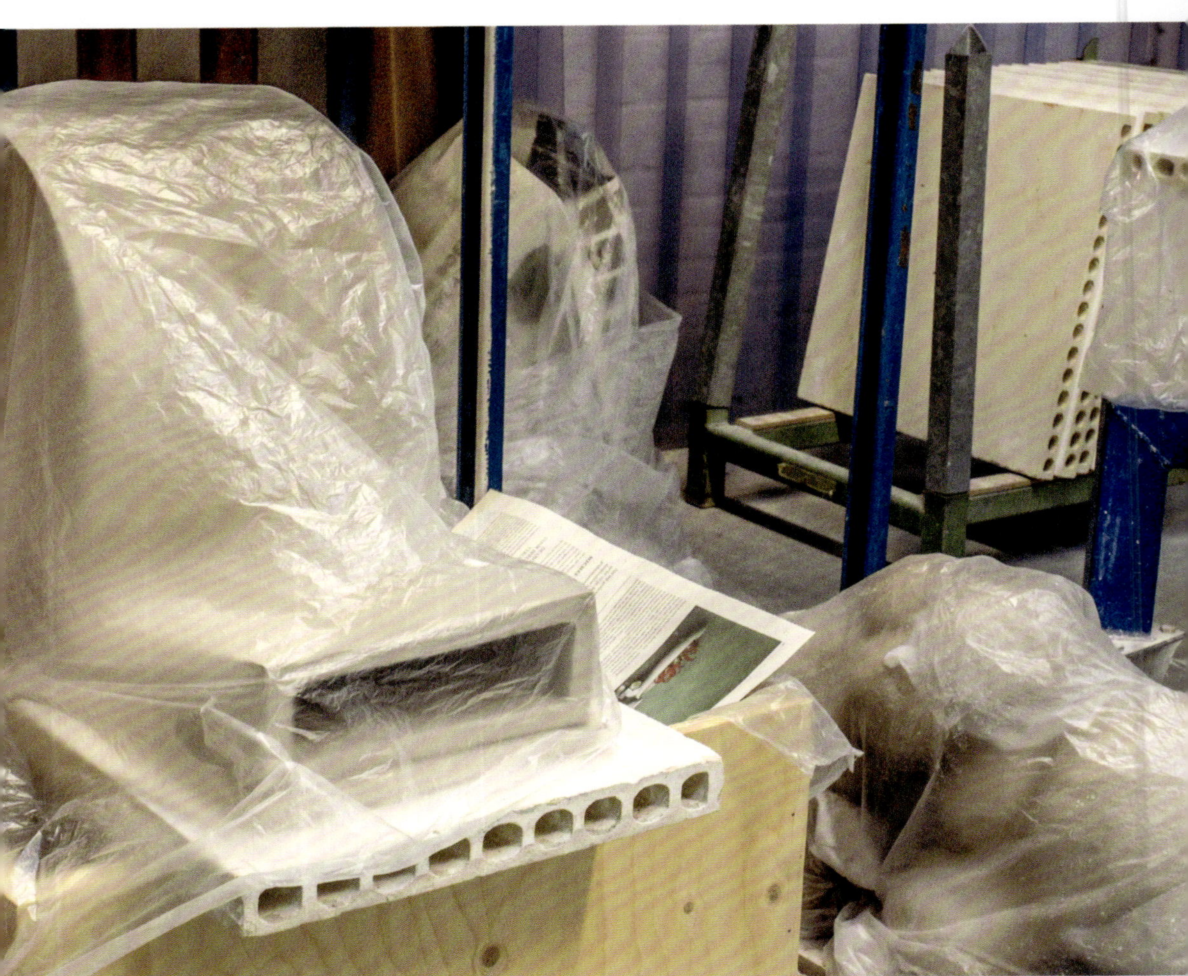

It is also worth mentioning that, in this show about memory, the personal histories of the advisors were of instrumental relevance. Some of them have been at Sundaymorning@EKWC for many years; they clearly remembered the making of the originals I asked them to ghost. This meant they had first-hand knowledge of the works' forming, of course, but also of the artistic intentions behind the projects. In recreating Breukers' *Big Bag*, for example, the decision was taken to use an actual shopping bag as a supporting structure, resulting in a different form to the original but matching its original conception. This was motivated as much by a sense of what Breukers himself might have liked to see done to his work, as by any pragmatic consideration.

Finally, in a few exceptional instances, the advisors granted themselves permission to radically alter the original work. Their two separate renditions of Christie Wright and Arjen Noordeman's project *Audiowear* (2010) – jewellery that doubles as musical instrumentation – are huge leaps from the original. Thanks to the 50-pound rule, a set of pan pipes originally of necklace scale has become an impressively iconic artefact, like some ancient archaeological find. More whimsically, the team decided to extract just one whistle from a necklace that originally had many of them, and stipulated further that the ghost version should be shown upside down. This decontextualization, along with the object's hard-edged contours, gives it the feeling of a wholly original abstraction. To me, it seems a genuinely new work inspired by the old, rather than just a spectral shade.

The advisors also took it upon themselves to ghost a work that was not on my checklist at all – they just thought it would be interesting (I won't say which one). In discussing these bolder moves with them, I was reminded that these are people who spend a lot of time in intense discussion with artists. Moreover, some of them trained as fine artists themselves, or even maintain an independent studio practice outside of their time at the Centre.

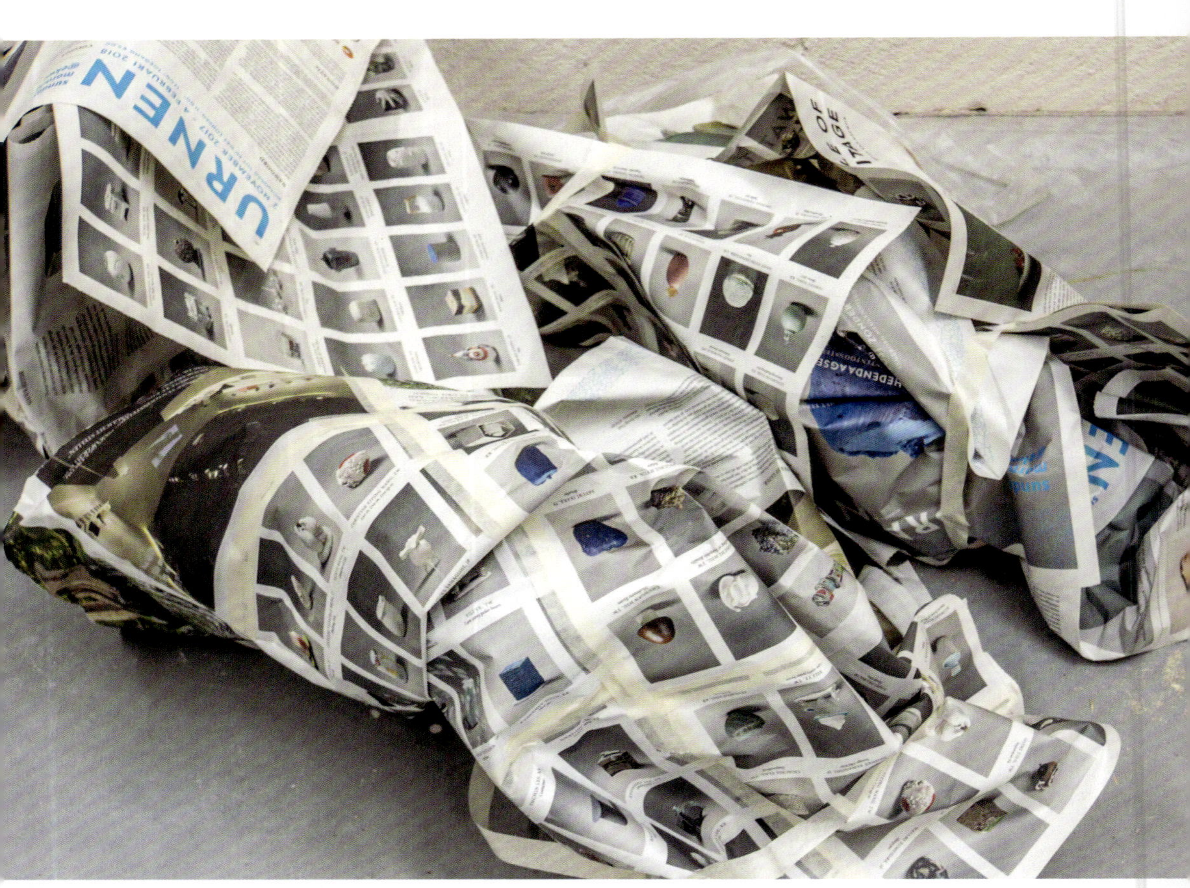

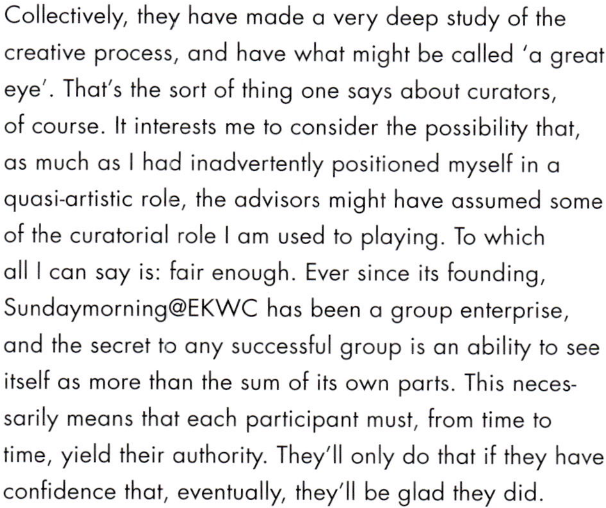

Collectively, they have made a very deep study of the creative process, and have what might be called 'a great eye'. That's the sort of thing one says about curators, of course. It interests me to consider the possibility that, as much as I had inadvertently positioned myself in a quasi-artistic role, the advisors might have assumed some of the curatorial role I am used to playing. To which all I can say is: fair enough. Ever since its founding, Sundaymorning@EKWC has been a group enterprise, and the secret to any successful group is an ability to see itself as more than the sum of its own parts. This necessarily means that each participant must, from time to time, yield their authority. They'll only do that if they have confidence that, eventually, they'll be glad they did.

In a very short space of time – like most people who come into contact with the Centre – I have come to feel deeply a part of it, and touched by its very particular magic. To be totally honest, this project is something I tossed lightly into the air, not knowing where it would land. I feel that I did very little – certainly in comparison with the advisors, who are always so in demand, yet somehow found the time to take on this heroic and collective act of making. This was conceived as an exhibition of and for the advisors. Ultimately, it's become an exhibition by the advisors, too. Whatever this project is, they are its true authors. I am willing to take credit for only one thing: I knew they had it in them.

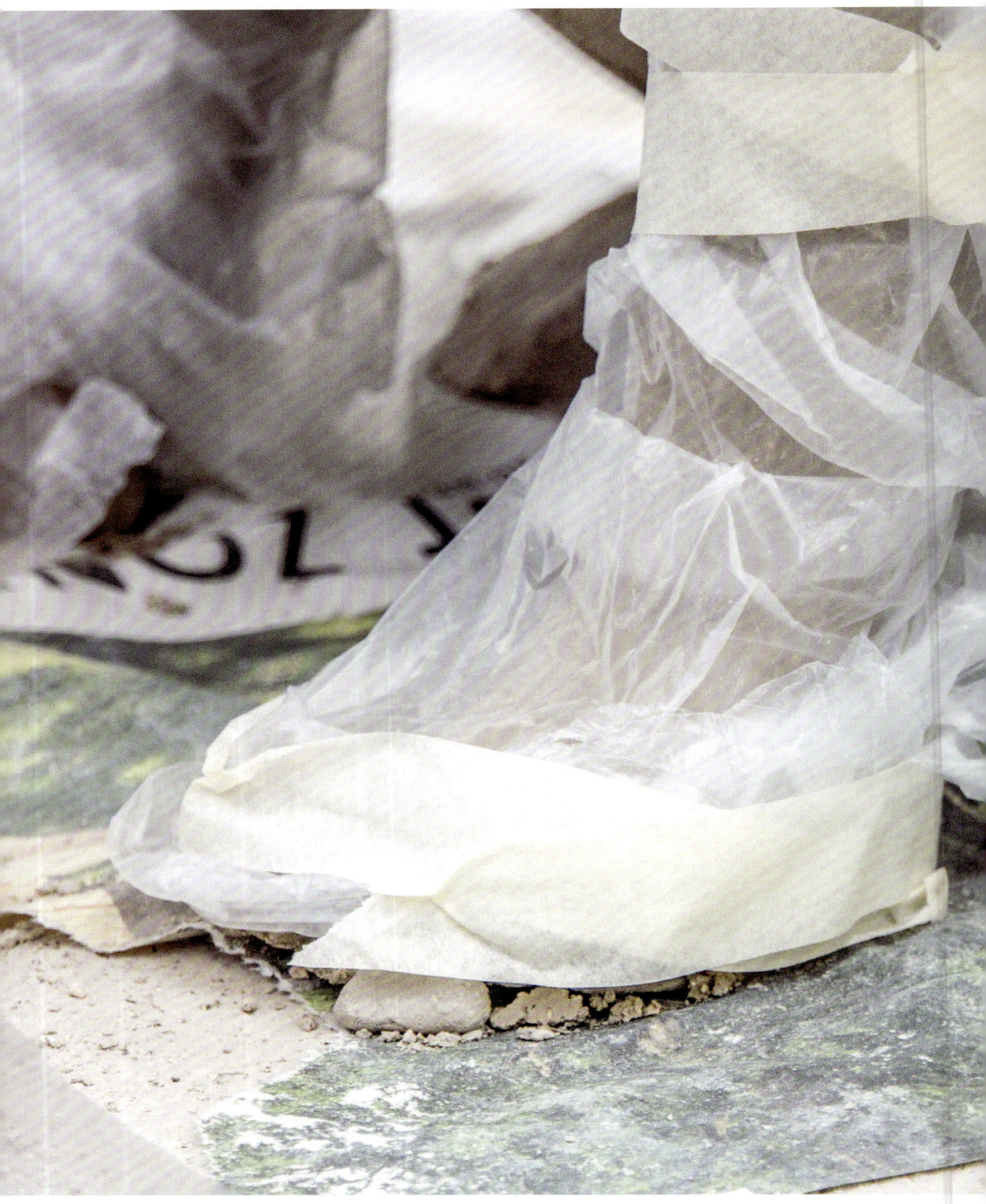

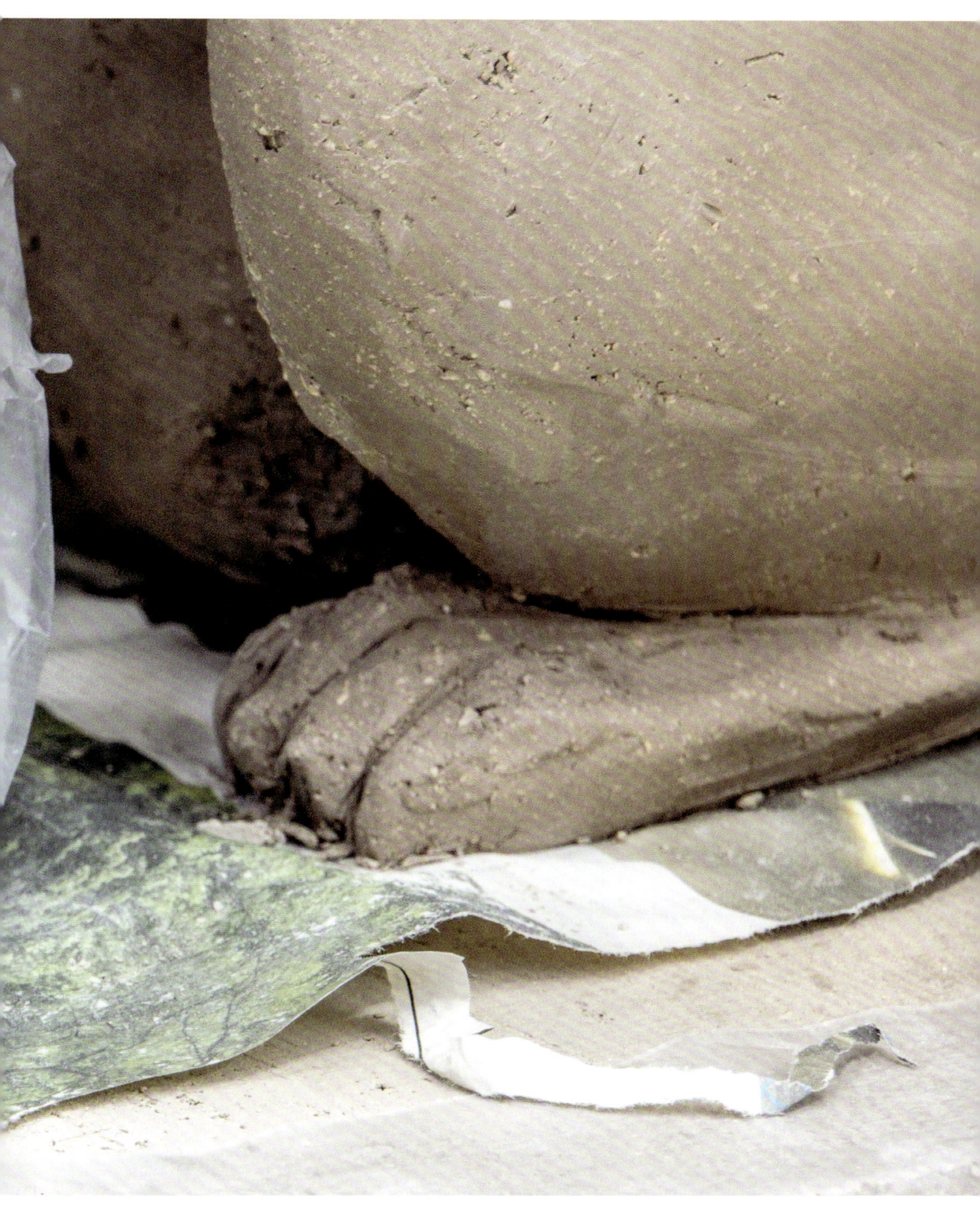

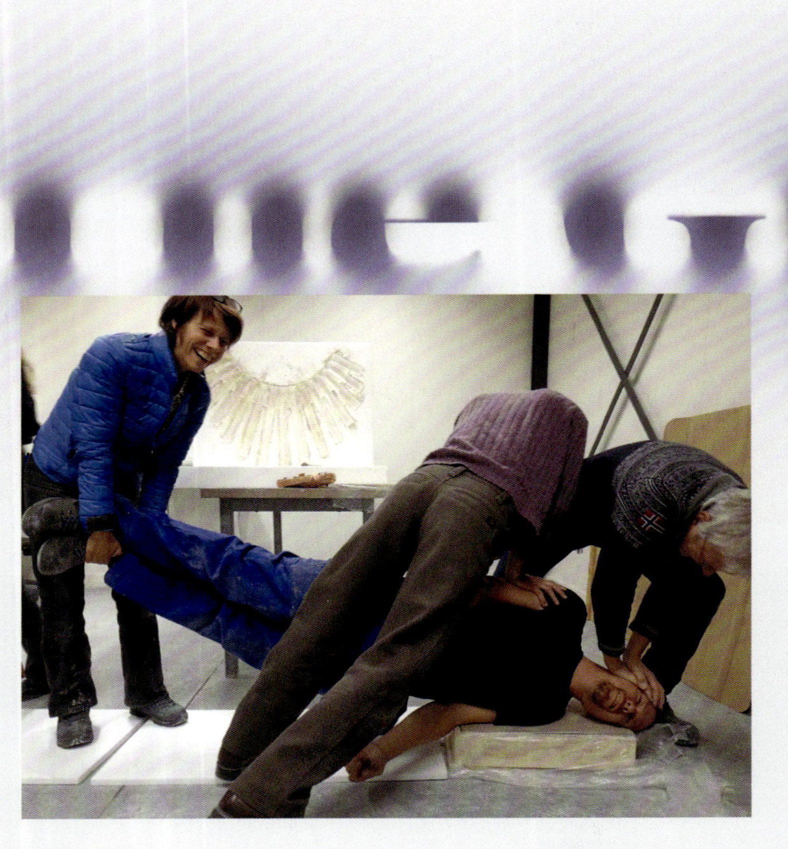

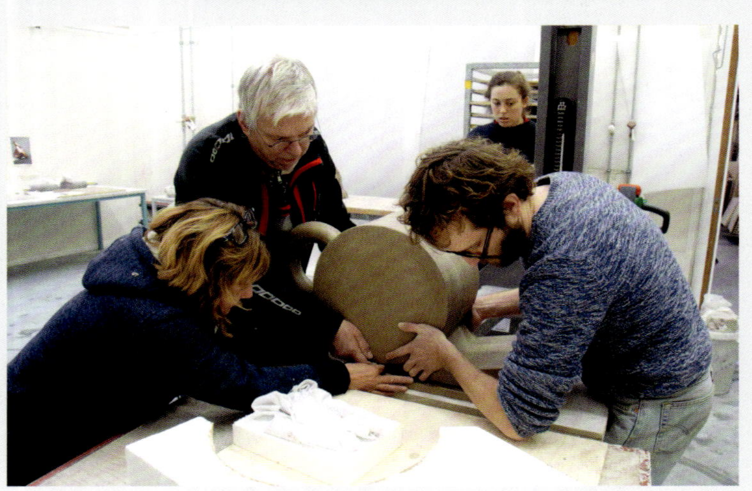

Interview with
the advisors

In January 2019, about halfway through the process of making Ghosts, curator Glenn Adamson sat down with the six advisors at Sundaymorning@ EKWC: Sander Alblas, Froukje Van Baren, Katrin König, Peter Oltheten, Marianne Peijnenburg and Pierluigi Pompei. What follows is an edited version of that conversation, which yields insights into the project as well as the unique role of the advisor.

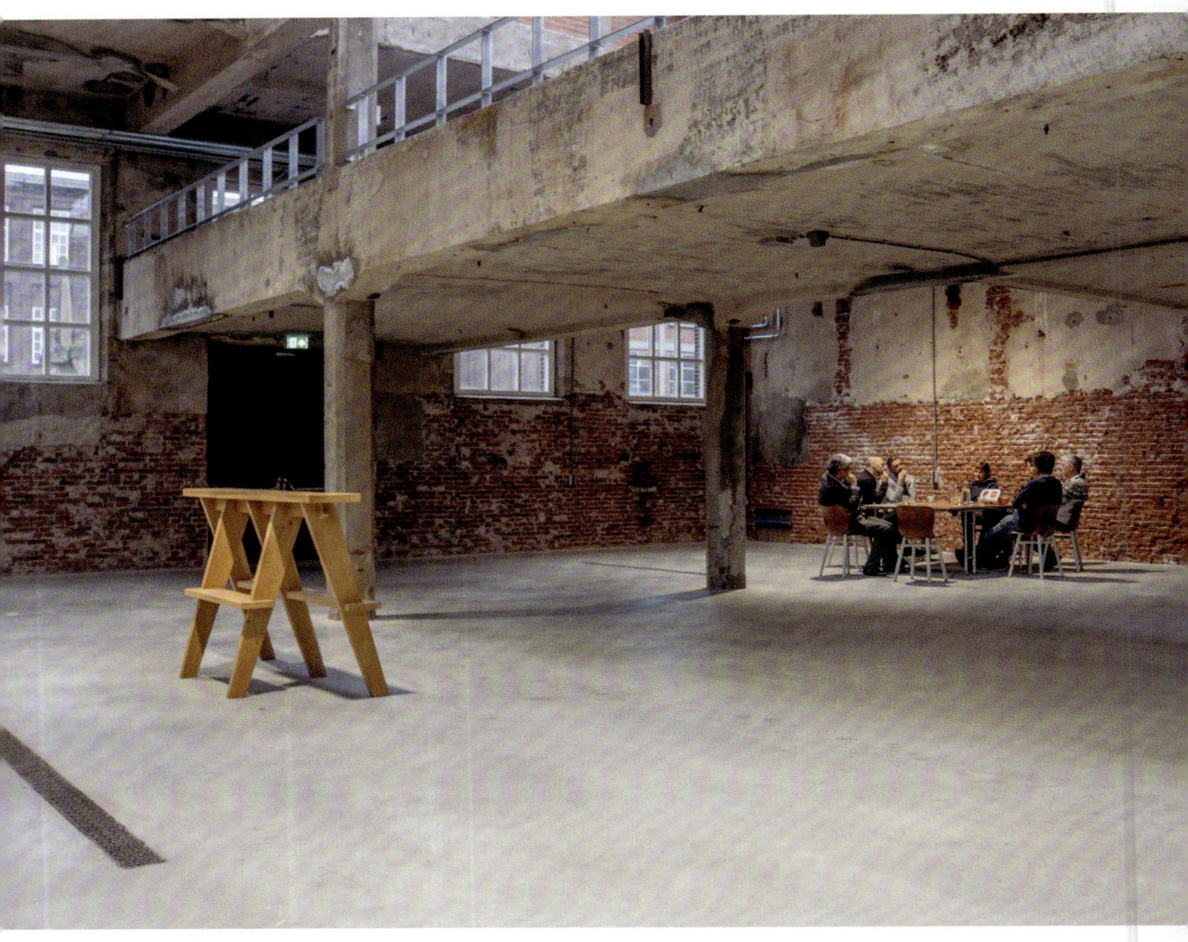

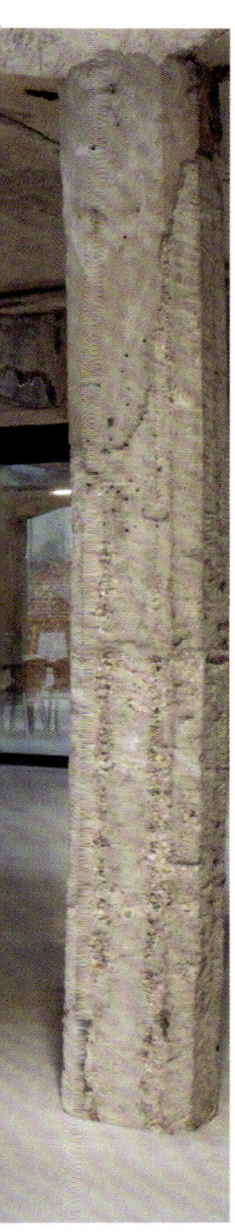

Glenn: Let's begin with introductions. Can each of you tell me something of your background and how you came to Sundaymorning@EKWC? Peter, let's start with you, as you've been here the longest.

Peter: I came in 1988, but actually I started as a little boy, digging in the earth. I figured clay out for myself: built my own wheels, then my own kilns. I made a lot of mistakes – very good mistakes, if you make them once. I worked for myself, too, in a little workshop – I didn't make a living from it. So I also worked at a factory, for four years. Mobach, in Utrecht. It's a little factory, but they make handbuilt pieces, everything is either wheel-thrown or slab-built.

Glenn: What was the Centre like when you arrived?

Peter: Then it was only the Ceramic Work Centre – no 'European' in the name – and it was in Heusden. I'd read about it. At that time I also worked at the art school in Breda, St. Joost, and I was in good contact with the leader of the Workshop. We bought things together, like pigments, clay or special tools. We could exchange tools if we needed. Then there came an advertisement in the newspaper: we're going to build the European Ceramic Work Centre. At that moment, at the art school, ceramics was really going down. I had only four students. That was no future for me, so I thought: 'I have to take my chance.' I went to the director and 'put my foot between the door', as we say in Dutch, and I said: 'If you want to build this centre you cannot do it without me. You cannot go around me.'

Glenn: In other words: 'I have to be part of it.' And later the Centre moved to Den Bosch, and in 2014, here to Oisterwijk. Can you briefly say what the transformation of the organization has been over that time?

Peter: So, I had my foot in the door and they accepted me, first for one afternoon a week, just to do maintenance, and then after three months they said: 'Okay, can you come for four days a week?' So I did that. At the end of the 1980s we started a different policy; he invited artists, not only the ceramicists from art school, but also artists, like sculptors or painters. And the work improved in quality, I think, by asking these artists in. So that was the first change, and then we moved to Den Bosch. Xavier Toubes, he was our artistic director at that time. It was a very nice facility there, very good. Then in 2012 the government cut our money supply. So we had to do something. Director Ranti Tjan came up with the strategy to move again, and he asked: 'Do you want to continue with me?' And we came to Oisterwijk.

Glenn: And here we are.

Peter: Here we are, yes.

Glenn: I understand you have a kind of leadership position on the team here, because of your seniority.

Peter: Officially I'm head of the workshop. But I try not to be. I try to decide together with the other staff members, because if you do that, you have a team. If you're the head of the team and always make the decisions, then it could work against you. I believe very strongly in that process, and I know that they all appreciate it.

Glenn: Before we go any further with the story, perhaps the others could introduce themselves.

Froukje: I came to the ceramic field at an advanced age (laughs). I was raised in France, and my first degree was as a 'technicien supérieur en Mesures Physiques'. I wouldn't know the exact translation for that, but it involved technical and engineering methods for measuring things, in all kind of fields: electricity, mechanics, some chemistry as well. This turned out to be quite useful later for glazing theory. In my mid-thirties I followed a course at the SBB (Stichting ter Bevordering Beroepsopleidingen) in Gouda, learning how to throw, handbuild, and the fundamentals of glaze theory. I realized this wouldn't give me enough training in the field, so alongside my regular job in social welfare, I applied for an internship at a ceramic enterprise called SteenGoed in Amsterdam. This had a dual purpose: giving psychiatric patients a professional working environment, and producing ceramics for several clients. After a few months this became my main job. I was employed as a production supervisor,

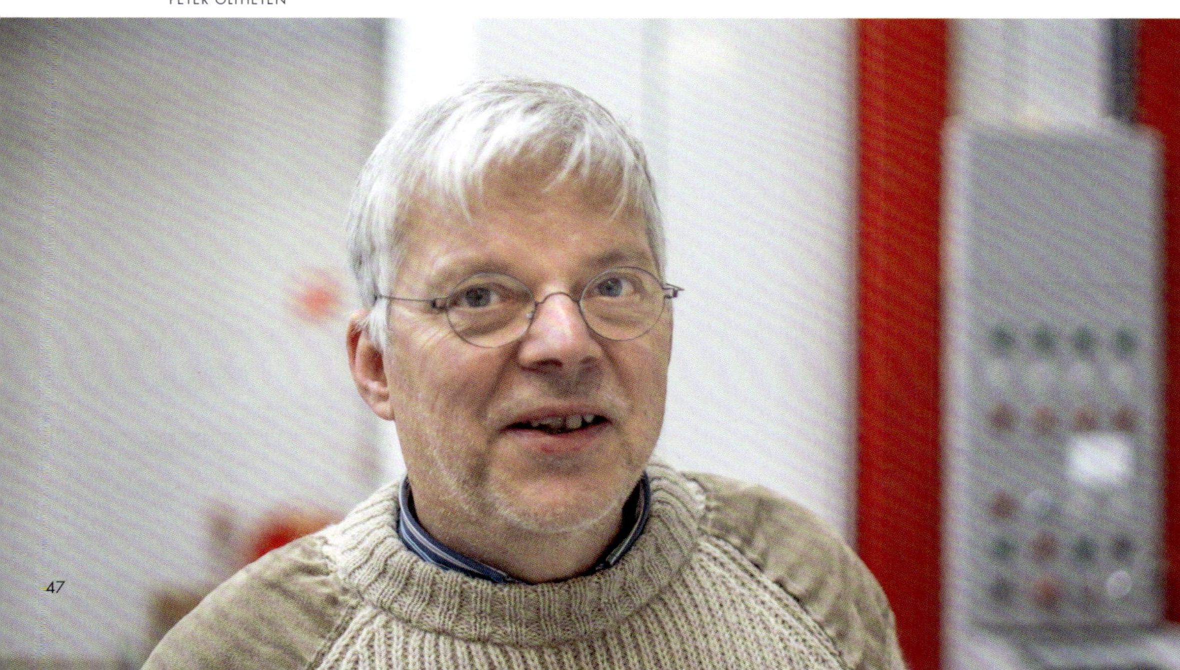

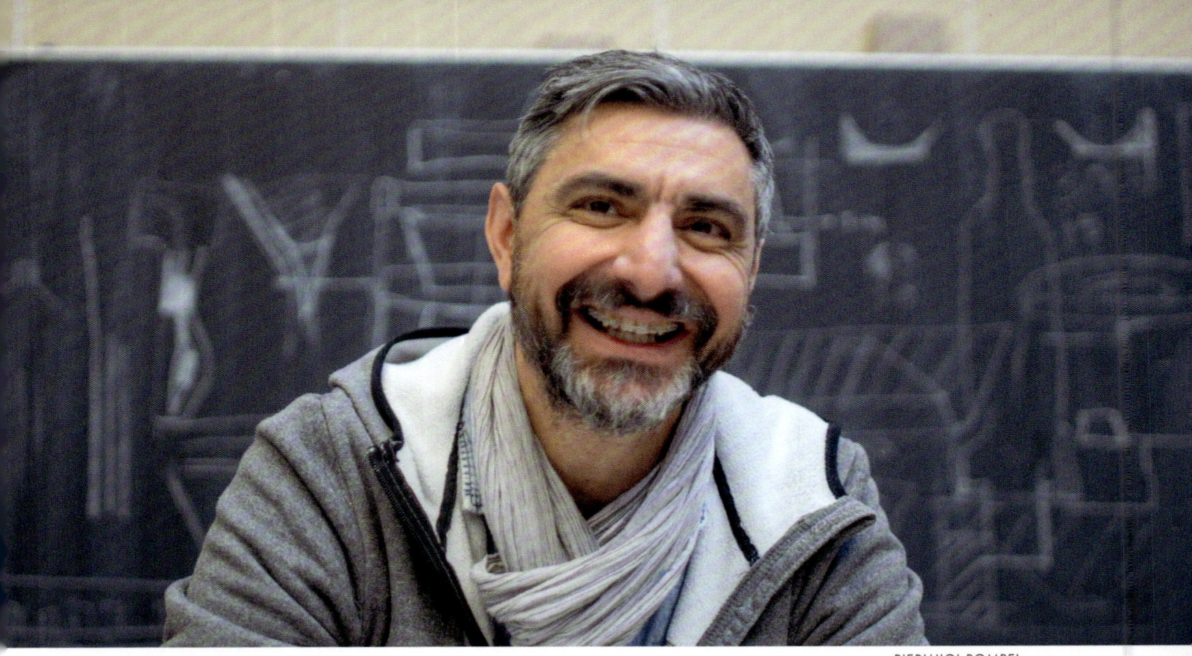

also working with the psychiatric clients/patients. I've been working here at the Centre for twelve and a half years now. I'm most often asked for assistance with glazing, but I also tend to give advice on making and drying.

Pierluigi: I'm a sculptor. I studied in Rome, and after I graduated I came to the Netherlands to, let's say, modernize my practice. I was very curious about changing the traditional background I had, so I studied here in the Netherlands and then decided to stay, because I found the artistic climate very interesting. I studied at the Royal Academy in the Hague, then started my career. My ambition was to come to Sundaymorning@ EKWC as an artist in residence when I finished school; eventually I succeeded, in 2006. I did a three-month residency and I must say I learned a lot, although I had a good background in making – my education in Rome was pretty traditional, so I knew about making moulds and stuff like that, but not specifically for ceramics. Then I did a second residency for a project called Brick, a collaboration among designers, architects and artists initiated by Koos de Jong. And slowly I developed a good connection with the colleagues here. Somehow we had the feeling that we could work together. So I was asked in to replace people

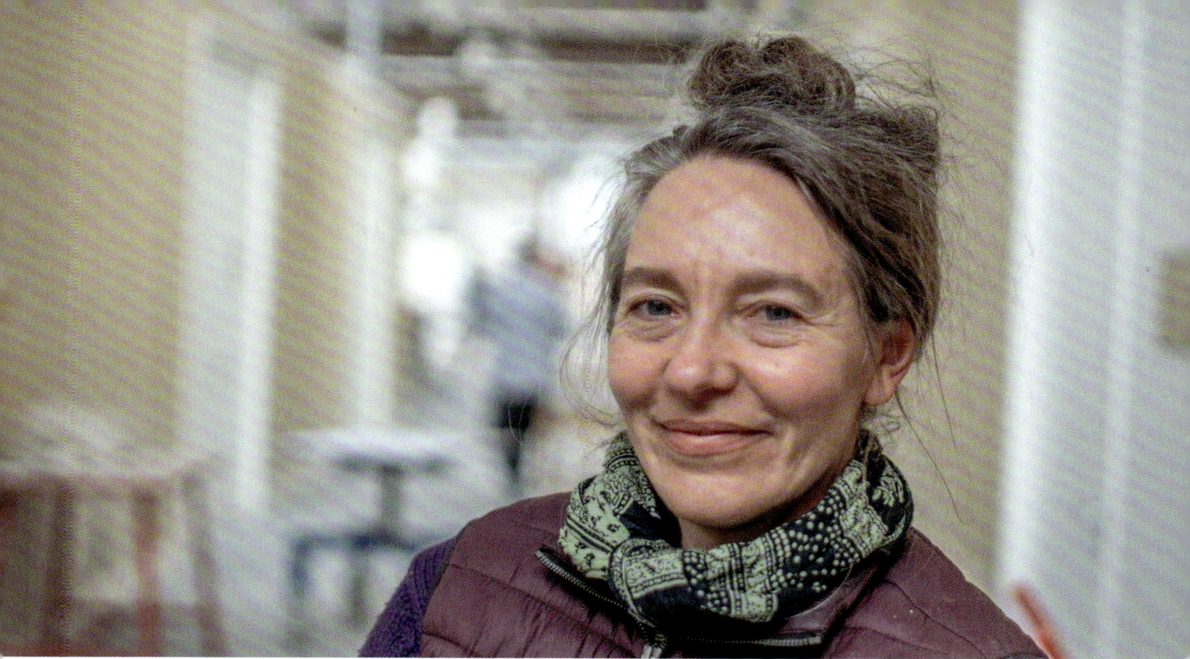

when they were ill, or were on maternity leave. Slowly
I became part of the team, almost on a regular basis.
And then in 2015 Ranti asked me to become a permanent member of the team. Parallel to all this, I also
teach at the Design Academy in Eindhoven and do some
guest teaching at the Rietveld Academy in Amsterdam,
the Royal Academy in The Hague and the St. Lucas
Academy of Fine Arts, Ghent.

Glenn: And you're still active as a sculptor.

Pierluigi: Yes. I must say that lately, I've spent a lot of
time on education and Sundaymorning@EKWC, so I'm
a little bit less active as an artist. But I think it's a kind
of flow, because already my hands are itching. I need
to make new work. So I had a kind of creative rest this
past year, and now I'll find a balance between the two
again.

Glenn: Do you think that your work at Sundaymorning@EKWC affects
your art, or are they separate in your mind?

**Pierluigi: The things that happen here definitely
influence my work, but it's information you try to leave
behind, because it's too much. It can influence your
behaviour, the way you think about your work. You do
think about the creative processes of the resident artists: where they start, where they hesitate. Sometimes
if I'm in my studio I think, like I'm mirroring, what's
the process they're going through? How do they solve
it?**

Glenn: It's as if you're constantly being presented with different models
of creativity, different rhythms in the studio.

**Pierluigi: Exactly. But when it comes to the visual
aspect, I try to forget it. I try not to get influenced. I'm
more interested in the process, the creative process of
the artist.**

**Katrin: I've been working in ceramics for more than 30
years. I have my roots in pottery, I learned how to make
thousands of pots on the wheel during my education in
Germany, especially in East Germany – it was at a high
technical level. I made pots for a lot of years and I also
worked in education. I educated other potters, worked
in Bolivia to set up a training centre for ceramicists,
giving classes to amateurs. And at the same time I did
my own stuff. I've been at Sundaymorning@EKWC for
more or less ten years; I came in with the same story
as Pierluigi, as a replacement for other colleagues,
and then I worked here for years every time when they
needed someone to come in at short notice.**

Pierluigi: Convenient for us.

**Katrin: Yes. I felt like a fireman. I worked like that for a
lot of years and for the last two years I've worked here
two days a week.**

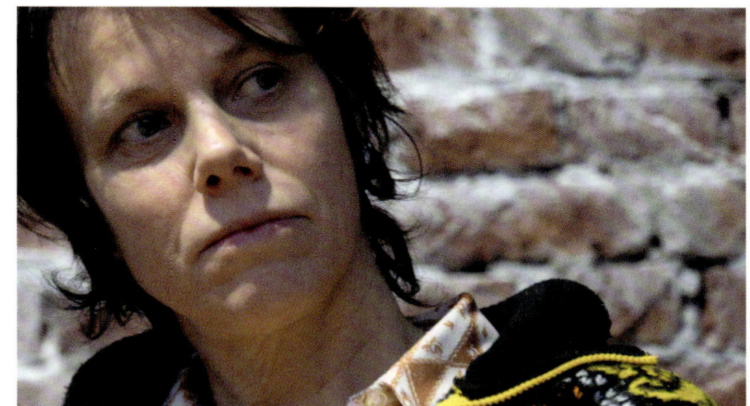

MARIANNE PEIJNENBURG

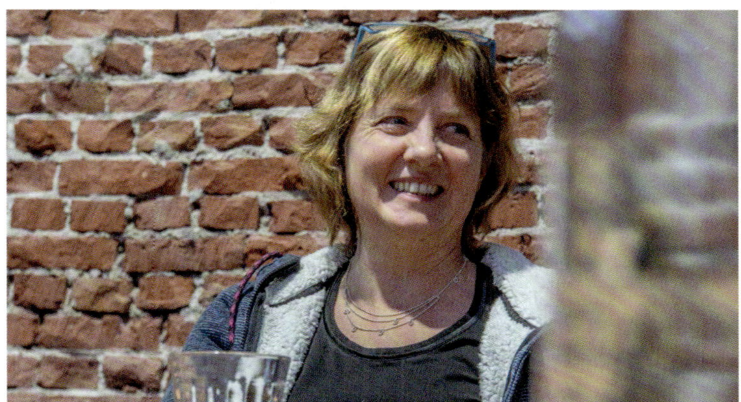

KATRIN KÖNIG

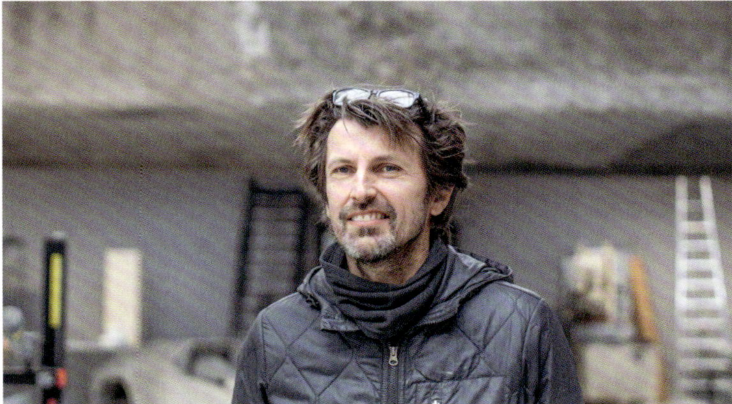

SANDER ALBLAS

Glenn: Are you still keeping up your practice as a studio potter?

Katrin: Life is going how life is going, so I stopped with table-ware and for the last three years I've been making bigger plates and wall objects. I also teach at IKKG (Institute of Ceramic and Glass Art) in Höhr-Grenzhausen, Germany.

Marianne: I'm a visual artist, in addition to working here, with no official education in ceramics. So I'm an autodidact. I learned ceramics while doing it at work, originally in a workshop for mentally disabled people. It was in a time in the Netherlands that they wanted mentally disabled people to have a more regular life, working at a job instead of being occupied. So there were about 60 people in groups, and they would do a bit of woodworking, a bit of cooking, all kinds of activities. And I had this group that worked a lot with wood and a little bit with ceramics. They couldn't operate the electric tools without me being in the room. I had to be there all day, changing saw blades, looking after people so they didn't cut their fingers and whatever. Then I said: 'Maybe we should change it around and do ceramics instead, because they can work on their own, without me being around.' So that's what they did and I had to learn the process of ceramics along with them, since I had to teach them, develop products and production methods to match their individual capabilities. The goals was to let them work as independently as possible. Because I didn't have a background in ceramics I made a lot of mistakes.

Glenn: Do you think that was a good way to learn? Through mistakes?

Marianne: Yes. Because you try a lot of things, and also come up with solutions that the books would say are impossible. Especially for coming here, that was a good way of learning.

Glenn: So then, how did you come to Sundaymorning@EKWC?

Marianne: At that ceramics centre we had several visiting artists. One of them worked at Sundaymorning@EKWC at that time, and so I found out about a position of instructor. It was basic things, teaching the artists in residence: how to make casting slip, how to make a glaze, all those things. And they hired me, and that's almost 17 years ago now.

Glenn: Sander, maybe we can move to you?

Sander: Well, I worked at a ceramics factory for quite a long time as an in-house designer. I was in charge of the decoration department. It was called Goedewaagen, it's in the north in the Netherlands. It was a very safe place, also a little bit isolated. So that was my world. The factory made a lot of small miniature houses for the KLM – the national airline. That was eventually transferred to China, but for a time there was a trajectory to introduce digital tools, like a milling machine. Their goal was to have an alternative for the traditional mould maker, to digitalize mould making. That eventually failed, because mould making is something you have to really know, and eventually this milling machine broke down. But it was my

introduction to CadCam. Then I did a 3D modelling course, on how to generate code for the machine and also how to operate it. At that time I met my present wife, who lived further to the south, and so I moved, but I was still connected to the factory. It was quite a long distance to travel, so I started working from home for them, just doing the digital preparation of files. Then one evening I was Googling, trying to find a job close to where I lived, and I kind of stumbled upon a vacancy at Sundaymorning@EKWC. And that's how I came here.

Glenn: What year did you join?

Sander: 2010, when the digital workshop was created.

Glenn: So there had not been much of a digital prevision here, before then?

Sander: There was a CNC mill before and a colleague who would give advice on digital production. And in 2010 we received a European subsidy so we could set up this new kind of workshop.

Glenn: What are your thoughts on the position of digital ceramics at the Centre? How does it all fit together?

Sander: I think there has been, and still is, a bit of tension. There are many reasons for this, but

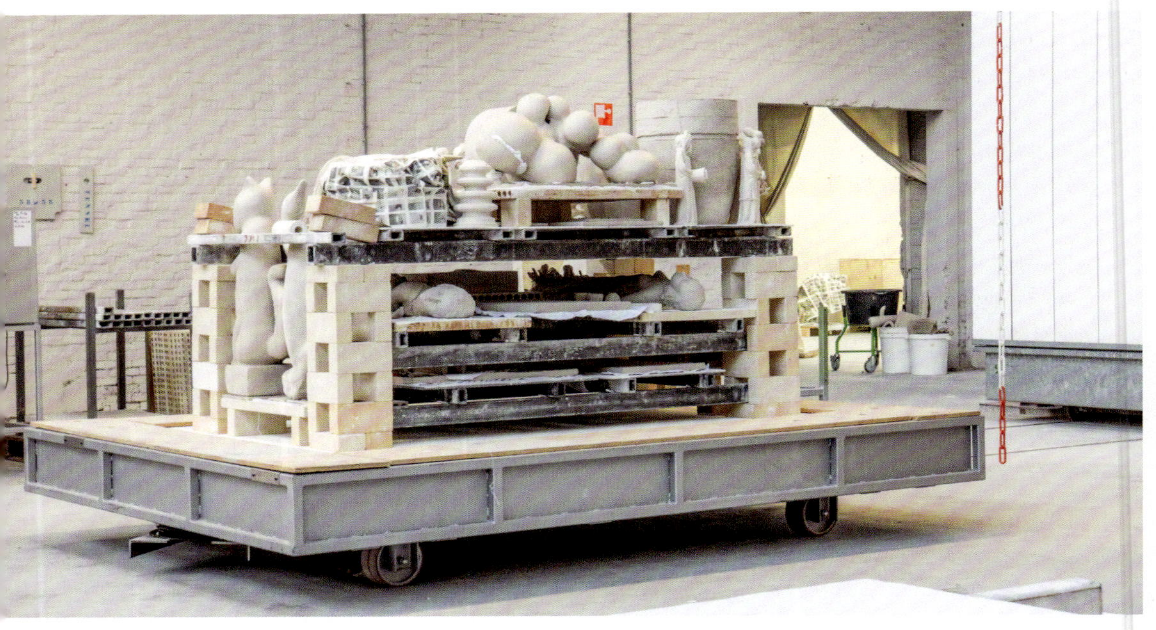

there is also of course an overlap. It's not really about
digitization itself, it's mainly about how to adopt a new
kind of tool into an already developed situation. The
tradition of mould making is of course quite old, while
digital mould making isn't. So it's a matter of trying
to adjust new tools to traditional ways of working.
And there is tension because it's not guaranteed that
it will work. I always say the 'E' in Sundaymorning@
EKWC stands for 'Experiment', and not so much for
'European'.

Glenn: Okay, thank you all for the introductions. Now maybe we
could start by talking about the role of the advisor here at the Centre.
Marianne, you've been doing it for so long, I wonder: How did you get
good at it? What was your path to competency as an advisor?

Marianne: Time. See a lot, ask a lot, see things go
wrong, make things go wrong and then read about it.
It's a constant circle. Every day here things come up
that I don't know.

Glenn: Are you very open with the residents about that? Do you tell them: 'Oh, I don't really know how to do that, but we'll figure it out?'

Marianne: Yes, and I'm also open with the colleagues here. Often you have a blind spot, and you can find a solution, but there might be something else you didn't think of. So I like to talk about it with Peter or Katrin or Froukje. 'How shall we do this? What do you think?'

Glenn: Do you also seek advice from outside the team here at the Centre? Other specialists who you call on?

Marianne: It's more the team here, but sometimes we might ask suppliers, particularly when they're outside of ceramics.

Glenn: And also for equipment maybe, like tools? The kiln manufacturer for example?

Marianne: Yes.

Glenn: But it sounds like for the most part you're a very self-sufficient group.

Marianne: I think so. And that's also because we have different backgrounds.

Katrin: It's about our open thinking. It's not very easy to find people who can leave behind standard solutions and come up with creative ones.

Froukje: You must be able to listen. Listen carefully to what somebody wants, and also to see if there's anything that might be innovative in the way of working. There are ways to do things that we already know, and then there are new ways to make things.

Glenn: Is that innovation important for the artist, or for the Centre?

Froukje: For both. It's important also to have joy for yourself. So there is always a challenge.

Sander: There's only so much time you can spend on a participant, but I also feel a need to do things that might not work perfectly. So I sometimes use participants a little bit as guinea pigs. It's the same story with a hospital and a patient: the patient needs the hospital, but the hospital also needs the patient, to increase the knowledge.

Glenn: Is there sometimes a decision point, when working with a resident, where you have to determine whether it will go down a digital pathway or stay on an analogue pathway?

Sander: Of course participants come with a question or a need. Sometimes it doesn't make sense to make it in a digital way, but there are many reasons why a participant might want to use digital fabrication anyway.

Often it's just curiosity. So then I
think: 'Who am I to say this is not
correct?'

Peter: People often ask me: 'Is this
possible?' And I say: 'It's possible.
If you also do that … and that …
and that.' For instance, if you want
to make a plate, you don't have to
throw it. It's possible to cast one,
or to press it in a mould.

Glenn: So you're often trying to find a way
around. Not the most obvious path, but a path
that will actually be easier.

Pierluigi: You can make things in
different ways, and sometimes
things are on the edge of what's
possible. So you might ask the
participant to do the experiment.
Because they are here, they have
time, they like to experiment, and
also in this way they will discover
new things, things that are unpre-
dictable. That's how we build up
our knowledge, I think.

Glenn: So for the participant it might be better
to use a more experimental technique, because
there's also more discovery and uniqueness, I
see.

Marianne: If it's not better for
the participant, then there's no
need for us to make them choose
the difficult way. It's not like that.
Only if it brings something to the
participant as well do we go the
experimental way.

Katrin: When we see that the participant is on an interesting path, but then decides not to go further, we sometimes do some tests ourselves, just to see.

Glenn: So you are extending what the participant is doing.

Marianne: And sometimes you have to take over part of the experimentation, because the participant is not reliable in his tests or the documentation of them.

Pierluigi: There is one important thing, though: the question is often not only on the technical edge, but also on the conceptual edge. For example, if someone wants to make an object without touching it, because that's the artistic idea: 'I don't want to use my hands.' So sometimes their artistic point of view is so specific or so extreme that it makes us think about other ways of doing things. That's one interesting thing about having people from different disciplines, like filmmakers or architects.

Katrin: Though when an artist comes in and says: 'I'll just make some plates,' I think: 'Oh, God.' Because plates are very difficult, it can take three months to get good plates.

Glenn: Do you think that artists who don't have a background in ceramics tend to take functional forms, like plates, for granted? Is there a kind of stereotype about pottery that people sometimes arrive with?

Katrin: At least with the European artists, yes. Asian artists can be different, but European artists sometimes think: 'It's nothing, it's just a plate.'

Glenn: Would you sometimes end up simply making the plates for them?

Katrin: Not in my role as an advisor.

Glenn: Why not?

Katrin: This is how we work at Sundaymorning@EKWC. I give them the tools to make it themselves, and if it's really not possible then I can say: 'Okay, you can hire me, or I'll give you an address of somebody who can do it for you.' But then if I do any of the making myself, I do it with the artist right there with me, and we look at the shape together: 'Okay, you like this curve? Or no, two millimetres more, like this.' Because otherwise it will be my plate and not the artist's.

Glenn: So you're trying to use your skill, but with the artist eye's and sensibility.

Katrin: Yes. Something really strange happened to me when I started to make new but really different ceramic work at home. Here at Sundaymorning@EKWC I carefully plan kiln schedules, and for my own work I don't. There was a moment when I had a colleague on the phone, I was crying with frustration because nearly everything had broken in my last firing. And she said: 'What's your kiln programme?' And at that moment I realized I didn't event think about writing an appropriate programme. I stopped the kiln and and I thought: 'Now I have to be my own advisor.' And wrote down for myself, I give you this and this advice. And then I tried to follow it. And it did work out.

Glenn: I understand that participants often

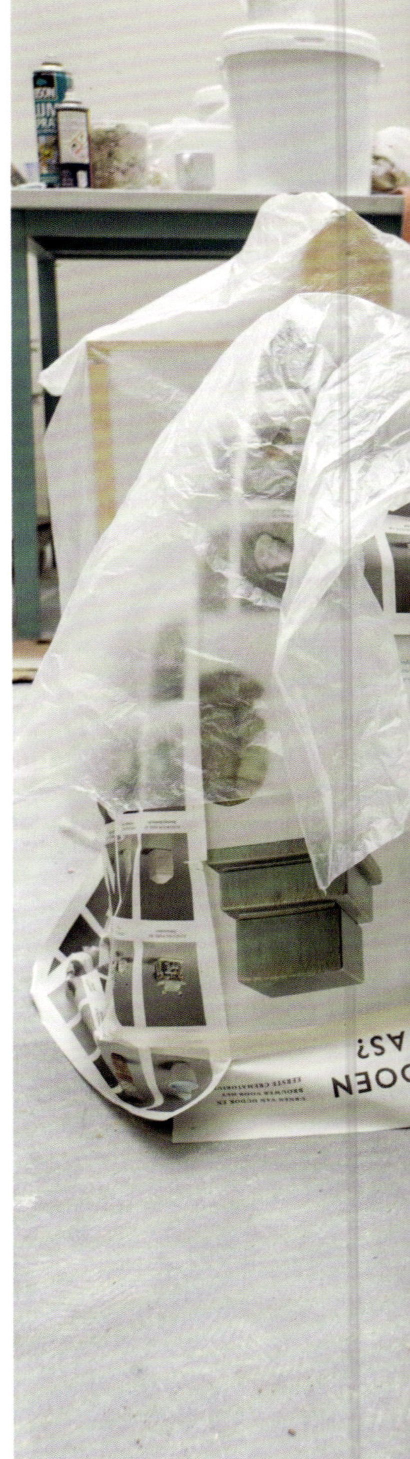

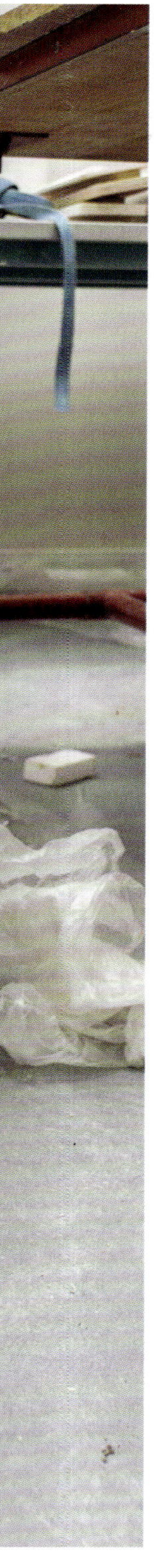

have a big shift in the course of their project. Can you all speak about that? What the rhythm of the 12 weeks tends to be like?

Pierluigi: It's different for each person. Some people know what they want to do at the start, and they ask very direct questions. Others take four weeks, sometimes even five, and you have to kick them awake and say: 'Come on, what's your plan?' The one rhythm that's always the same is at the end: running out of time.

Katrin: In the kitchen, you can look around and tell how long each person has left: three more weeks, the last week, you can see it. Tired people and not enough time.

Glenn: Do you think the relationship between the advisor and the participant is very psychologically intense?

Marianne: Could be. It's so different, there's not really . . .

Katrin: . . . yes and no. You try to react individually to each person.

Peter: But I think we are psychologists to some extent. We have to nurse, we have to take care of them.

Katrin: And sometimes you have to play mama a bit, too. Like: 'Do you sleep enough? Have a nice Sunday. Go out.' Not with everybody of course, but sometimes.

Pierluigi: I also know, because I've been a resident myself. You need to give them attention, you have to take care of them. You see when they are in a kind of panic mode,

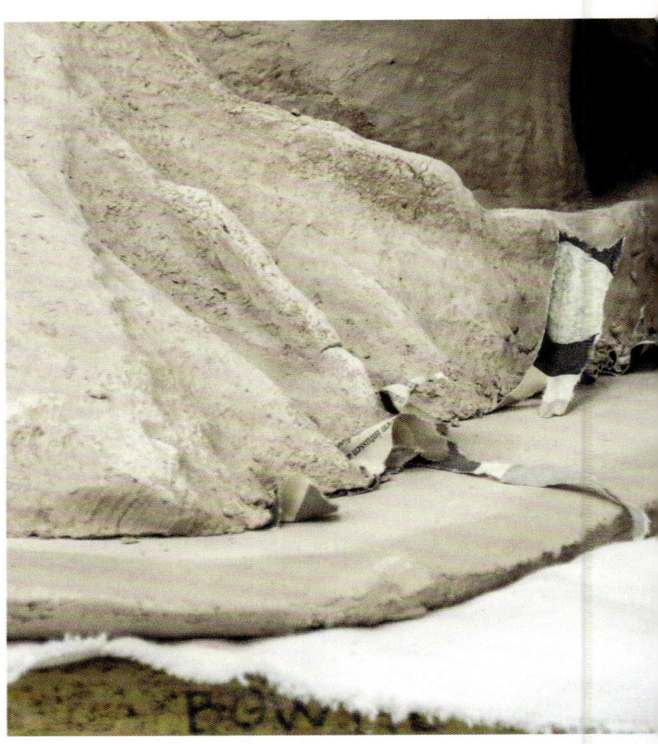

like they don't know what to do, or they are very excited. But it's
very subjective, because a lot of artists are very self-confident
and they are sure about what they're doing and we don't see them
hesitating. Other artists need a lot of advice, and whenever you
are here, you have to say hello, visit their studio, otherwise they
think: 'Is something wrong?'

Katrin: I think we don't talk about it, but each of us has a different role.

Glenn: Sometimes you will actually shift a participant from working with one of you
to another one, is that right?

Marianne: Sometimes it doesn't work, the advisor and the resident don't go together well. Then it's natural that somebody
else takes over, but on the other hand residents can also have a
preference, and that might change over the residency as well.

Katrin: When you ask one of us you always get a different answer.
It's never the same. Ceramics is so complex, it's not black or
white, it's grey. I always say: 'Please ask my colleagues and enjoy

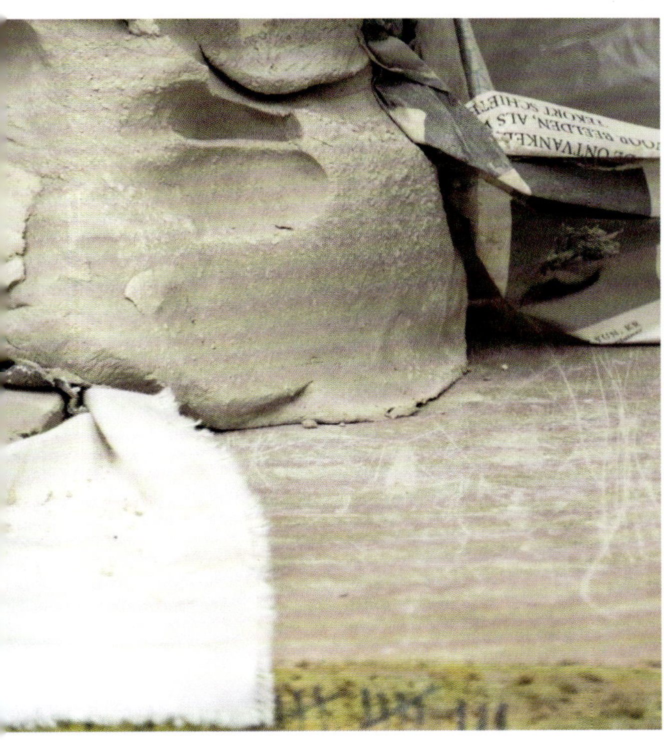

**the different answers. And then
you choose the best way for you.'**

Glenn: So there isn't one right answer – there
are just different answers. Can we maybe
shift now to the *Ghosts* project? What do
you think about the idea of an exhibition that
foregrounds your role as advisors, and puts the
emphasis on you as makers, rather than the
artists?

**Peter: We become more part of
the party, I like that.**

**Katrin: It's a different role. In the
beginning I had a lot of difficul-
ties, it was not possible in one
day to work two hours on *Ghosts*,
switch over to being an advisor,
and then to go back.**

**Marianne: In a way I like it, but
in practice it's more difficult,
and that's also a time issue. A lot
of the ghosts, they're made by
assistants and interns that we
advise. So then there is a different
role with the object, but it's still
not made by us.**

**Sander: Myself, I don't really see
much difference actually. In the
lab I do a lot for participants, in
terms of making. That's a difference to the other workshops,
because it would take too much
time for me, or for them, to teach
them software or how to use the
machines. So with the ghosts I'm
just milling moulds like I mill
moulds for participants. The convenient thing is that I'm also using**

**a mould that I previously made for a participant, from
his original work. I can enlarge it or make it smaller or
whatever.**

Glenn: Oh, really? You still had the mould?

Sander: I have a digital file, a ghost file.

Katrin: You are the ghost.

Glenn: So in some cases you have just a black-and-white image, not
much to go on. And at the other extreme you might have all of the
original information. Pierluigi, what do you think about the idea of
being put on stage as an advisor?

**Pierluigi: I was very surprised, in a positive way. When
you have a 50-year-anniversary, I don't know, I was
expecting to have masterpieces coming back in an exhibition. But this is really about us. So I think it brings
quite a lot of value to what we do.**

Glenn: I would love to hear more about the process of capturing the
work. It's so different to have the piece sitting in front of you and
making a copy, but if you only have an image – you might have to
imagine what the back might look like for example. Can you talk a little
bit about that?

**Pierluigi: I didn't understand the idea at first. I won-
dered, am I supposed to look for other images? I
thought I should, so I mailed the artist. But she only
had very vague images, not really useful. Because it
was something figurative, a dog, I could find other
images of dogs. I think if I would go further now, knowing that that only one image should be the one that is
inspiring us, then I would stick to that and try to figure
it out through my own interpretation.**

**Pierluigi: I've tried to look for work that was a little
bit challenging. As a mould-making specialist I always
use slip clay, but in one particular case I thought: 'I'll**

handbuild something.' It would be nice for me to try
something different. I struggled with the picture, trying
to catch the soul of the work, that was really hard, but
a nice experience. The creative process is just as difficult as when you deal with your own work. It comes
from the picture, but you're making something, so you
cannot separate the hand from your heart. You still try
to put your own eye and soul into it. So I experienced it
as exactly the same process as making my own work.

Glenn: Katrin, would you agree with that?

Katrin: Yes, I agree with him. At least in one case,
it was even harder than making my own work. The
sculpture by Harumi Nakashima, with the blue spots
on it. I had only seen this photo, never this work in real
life. I started copying it, but it was nearly impossible. In
a photo you can't see the depth. I asked my colleagues:
'What do you think?' and at a certain point we decided
to just make a sculpture, a good sculpture from it.

Glenn: What does a good sculpture mean? Just pleasing to your own
eye?

Katrin: We did it together . . .

Pierluigi: . . . we were trying to find the right balance,
the in-between space. It was more a visual process, to
try to catch the essence of the work, which was in the
picture, but then make it 3D.

Katrin: So we added two extra balls.

Glenn: You actually changed the design of it?

Katrin: With the right amount of clay, the 50 pounds,
it didn't look right. So we had two options: start over
– but we didn't have the time – or option number two,
make this ghost a better sculpture.

Pierluigi: I think it has to do with the character, so when you see the picture, you see a certain aesthetic, but you also see a certain language. Although you don't know what's behind it, we basically try to adhere to the same language.

Marianne: I made one or two that I know how they were made. If you know the idea behind it, you can take a different approach. One of the things I made was Tim Breukers's *Big Bag*. It wouldn't make sense on a smaller scale – to make a small *Big Bag* – because I know he would never do that. It's not how he works. So I made a sculpture with a shopping bag, because with the weight of the 50 pounds, that would be the size of bag you would have. So you have the same principle of making the work.

Froukje: Each Ghost is made of 50 pounds of clay, but you still have to work out how big the piece will be. When you've seen other pieces, made of the same amount of clay, you have an approximate idea, but while you're working you have to think – will it be over or under? So that was quite a constraint. I was making a Johan Creten (*When Owls Become Parrots*) and all I had was two pictures, one in profile and one from the front, so I had to make a lot of guesses.

Glenn: Originally he cast it in a mould?

Froukje: Well, Creten made an original and then he made a rubber mould from it, and then made changes to that mould. I tried to follow the imprint of the image the best I could, but didn't try to get into Creten's skin to make it. I just tried to focus on what it looked like. When you try to remake it, you just try to see the ratio of different parts, but the signature is still different. I made it at home and I didn't have very much distance to have a good look at it, so the first time I made the head, it was far too big.

Glenn: It's like a sculpture of a sculpture. What do you think of it, now that it's finished?

Froukje: Well — it's something I put some effort and time and attention into. I know it has my signature, but I can't do otherwise. It's my hands making it, not Creten's, so there comes out something that is from me. But it's also not me, and it's not mine.

Glenn: Was there a technical reason that you chose this one to make? Does it correspond to your skill set?

Froukje: It was more that this is the way I like to work. I think that's how we all chose our pieces.

Glenn: Rather than liking the work of art necessarily as a work of art, it was more about what you would actually need to do.

Froukje: Yes, and what would be a challenge to make, also.

Glenn: It sounds like there's a shifting basis on what constitutes truth to the original, and what you're trying to achieve, depending on what the original was and how it was made, as well as how much information you have. So each one of the Ghosts is kind of its own story.

Peter: Katrin and I worked together to make the Tony Cragg (*In Camera*). First I just threw a sphere, because I haven't worked on the wheel for years. And I thought: 'It's more or less okay. Can I make it thinner?' And then she did one. 'Let's do one of four kilos. Let's do one of three – no, that's too small.' In the end she threw three spheres of around four kilos each, that was the right amount. And then we adjusted everything to that scale.

Glenn: And were you working with Katrin because she's the stronger thrower?

Katrin: We have enough work here – it's not that we don't know what to do with our time – so with this Ghosts project, we would like to get something extra from it: it's one thing to work together in making and another is to have fun playing with the material!

Peter: We made an appointment on a day off. No artists tapping on your shoulder. Well, of course they did, but I said: 'I'm not here. I'm a ghost.'

Glenn: When you're making the 'Ghosts', it's a very different role then when you're working as an advisor. Do you think that the two things have something in common?

Peter: No. I think when you work on Ghosts you feel more free, because you have to do it yourself, working together with your colleagues, but you are playing. While when you are in the studio with an artist you try to go deep into the spirit of the artist. What do they want, and what's the best way to get it out of them? And now you just play.

Katrin: The Ghosts are made with our hands and working as an advisor is really about thinking, thinking, talking. I have to follow the thinking of the artist into his own world. This is a very big difference.

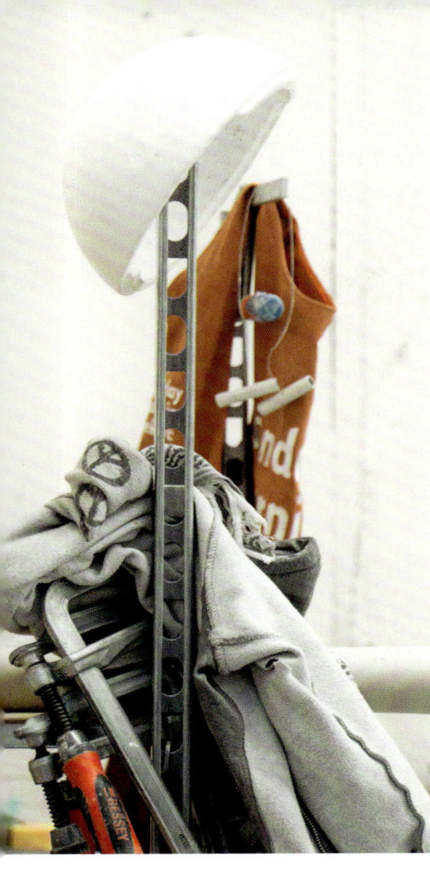

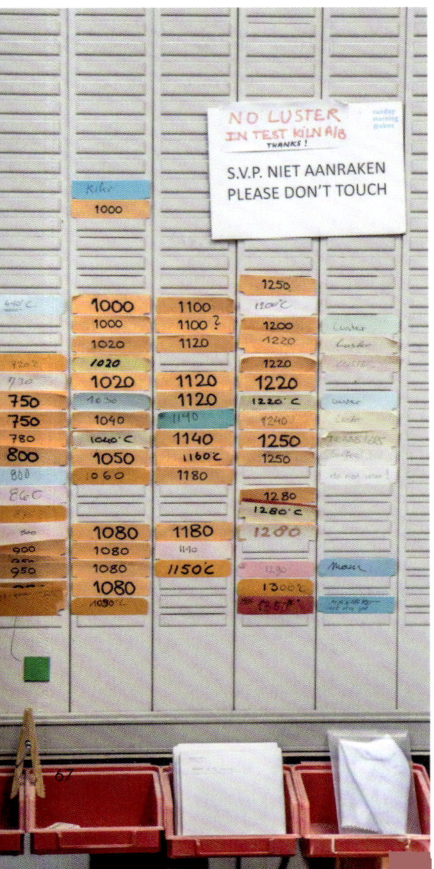

Marianne: And what's very important is that in our advising role, you never know what the outcome is going to be. There's no object yet, no work. And now we have the end work as the starting point. It's never like that.

Katrin: As an advisor it's open-ended. And now we start from a fixed end.

Pierluigi: For me it's a little bit different. It's not that it's a conflict, but a kind of parallel life: you have your own practice as an artist, and then as an advisor, and as a teacher. So I feel that my own artistic identity is split. Although I said it I was very into making the Ghosts, I don't know if I would put my signature on them.

Glenn: That connects well to the last thing I wanted to ask. Now that the Ghosts are actually almost finished, what do you think of them as objects? How do they seem to you as a group?

Sander: I'll only be able to tell when I really see them. They're all covered in newspapers now. I need a kind of overview, it's just a lot of different objects from a lot of different artists in a lot of different sizes. Once you have them all fired and glazed with a white cover, then you can see the connection. Right now, I don't see any connection.

Peter: We won't see until the day of the exhibition. We can imagine; the sculptures are in our heads, or in the pictures, all in colour. Katrin was talking about the sculpture with the blue dots, now the dots are gone. Or a dripping piece from Jun Kaneko is not dripping anymore, it's all white and very matte. I have to see it when the white coat is on and I think that will give a value to them. But I'm not sure if it will work at all, the pieces. We have to see.

Glenn: This is interesting, because maybe it actually is like what the residents are doing; you're not sure what is going to happen. This is one reason why I thought it would be interesting to do this project, because the status of the objects is so unclear. They are not really works of art. Like you were saying earlier, Peter, it's almost like they were designed by a ghost, or just by the situation. Each one is very specific, and at the end they are all there, and you have to step back and ask: 'What are these things?' It's an experiment that seems very true to the spirit of the Centre. So one last question: We haven't decided what should happen to them at the end of the show. Do you guys have any ideas about that?

Marianne: Just knock them into a container.

Katrin: Destroy them.

Glenn: Why do you say that?

Katrin: Because they are not clear, they are not our pieces. I think it's only about the process.

Marianne: They are made for a special purpose and they have served that. I don't see a need for them to stay around forever.

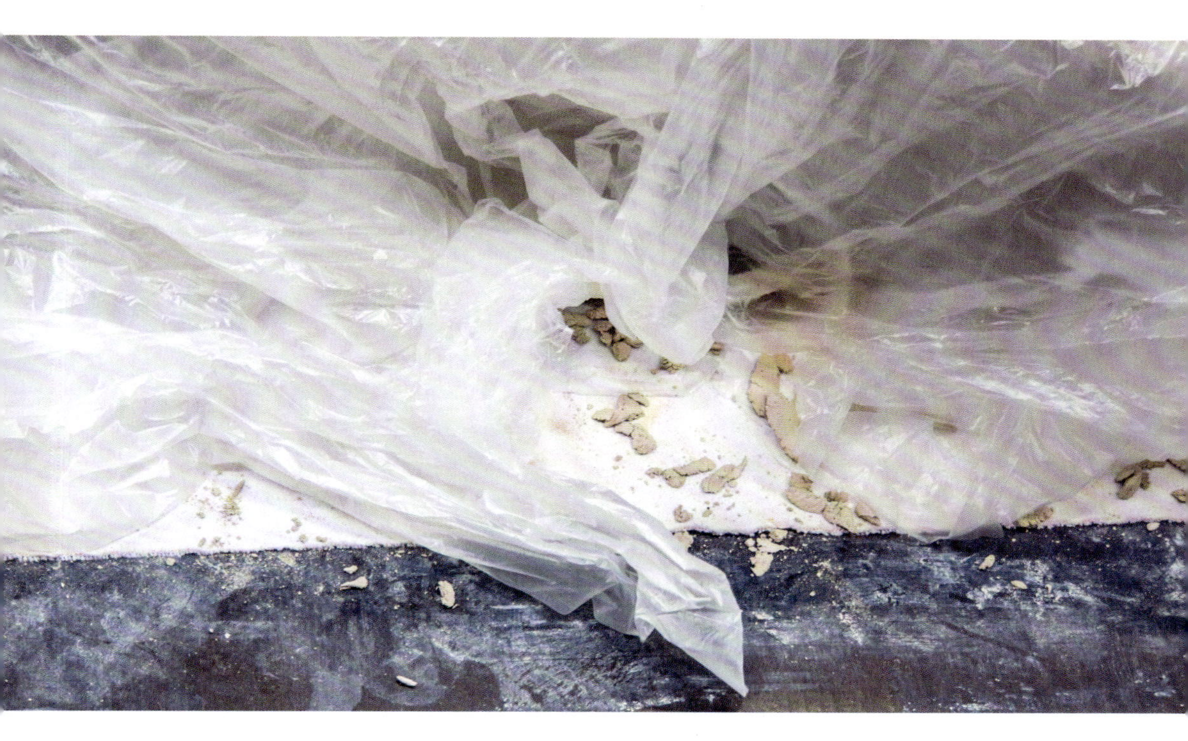

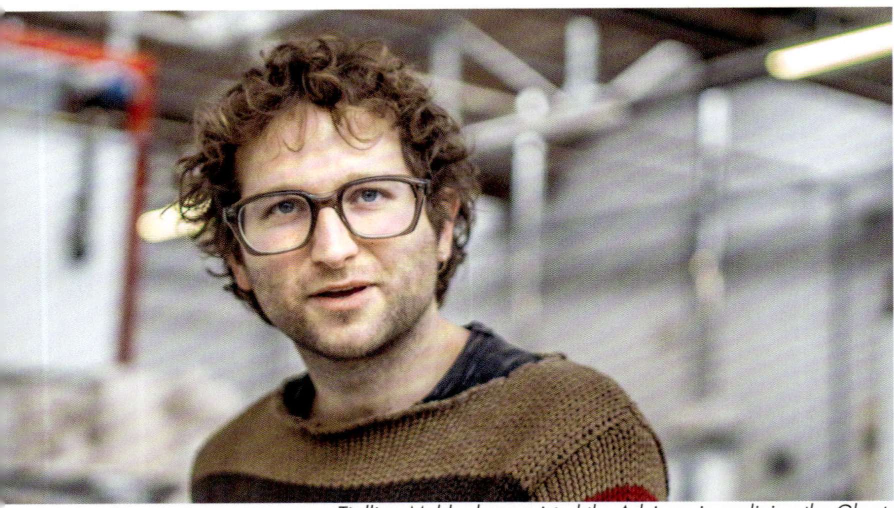

Tjalling Mulder has assisted the Advisors in realizing the Ghosts

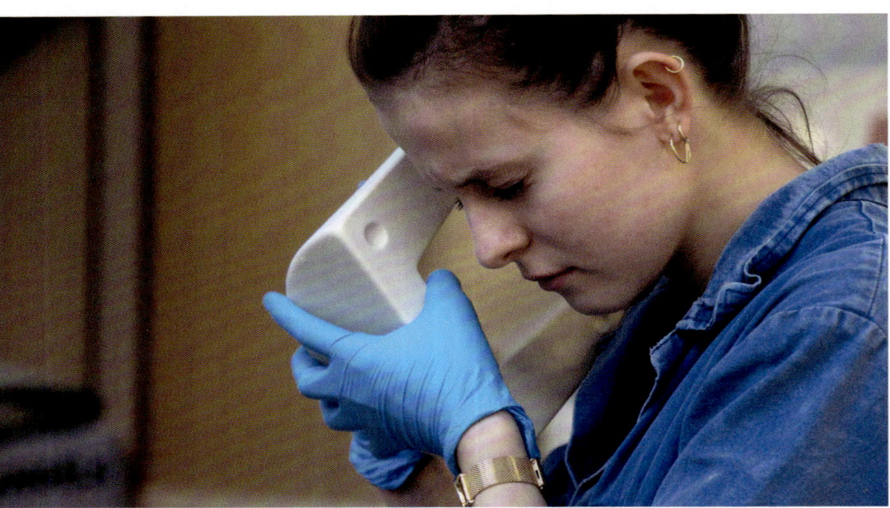

Rinke Joosten, assistant on the Ghosts project

Sander: I think we should sell them at Blokker.

Pierluigi: Well, personally I would like to keep mine. But I think they are definitely stronger when they are together.

Peter: It could be a permanent exhibition here, we have a lot of space.

Glenn: It tells you a lot about them, that this whole range of possibilities seems appropriate: anything from throwing them in a container and smashing them, to having them be a permanent memorial, to sticking them in a home goods shop.

Peter: Or you put them together, not for ages, but you put them somewhere in the corner for a year.

Marianne: And at the end of the year you destroy them.

Peter: Or just one of them. Every year one drops out: into the container. And so at the end, after 28 years, the last piece is gone.

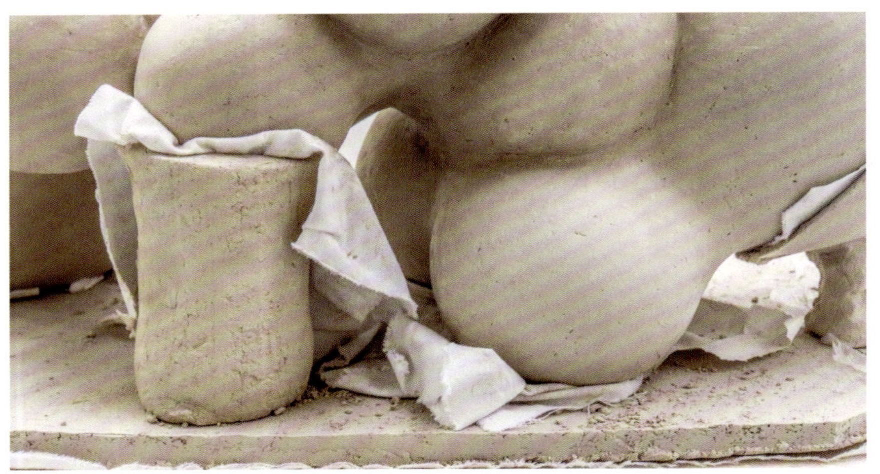

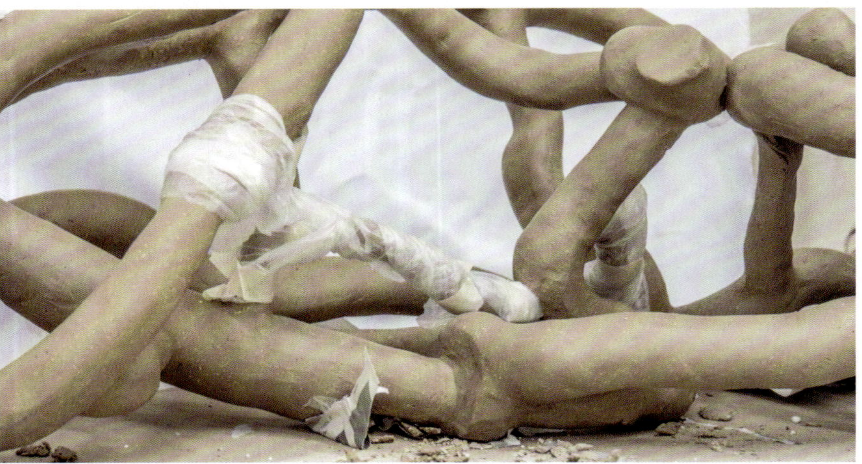

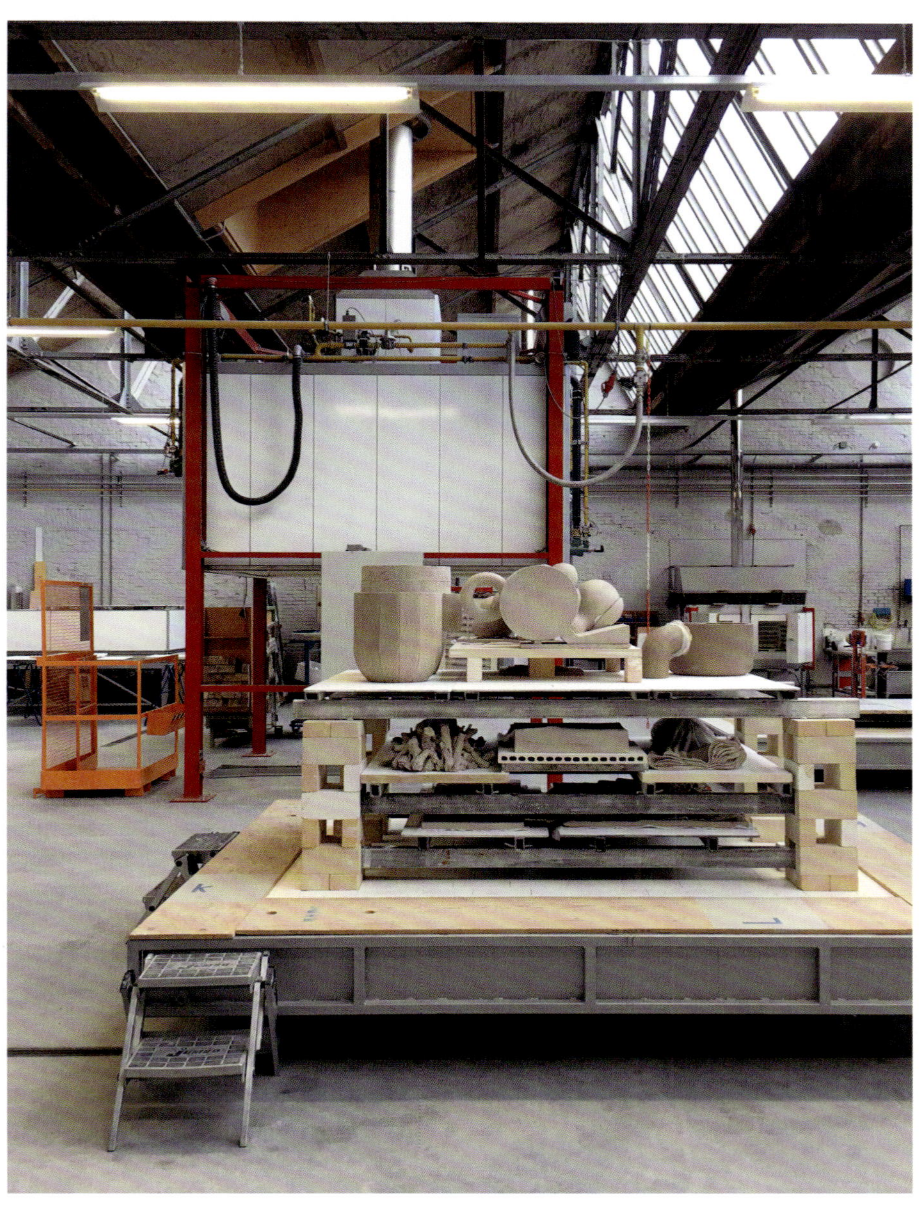

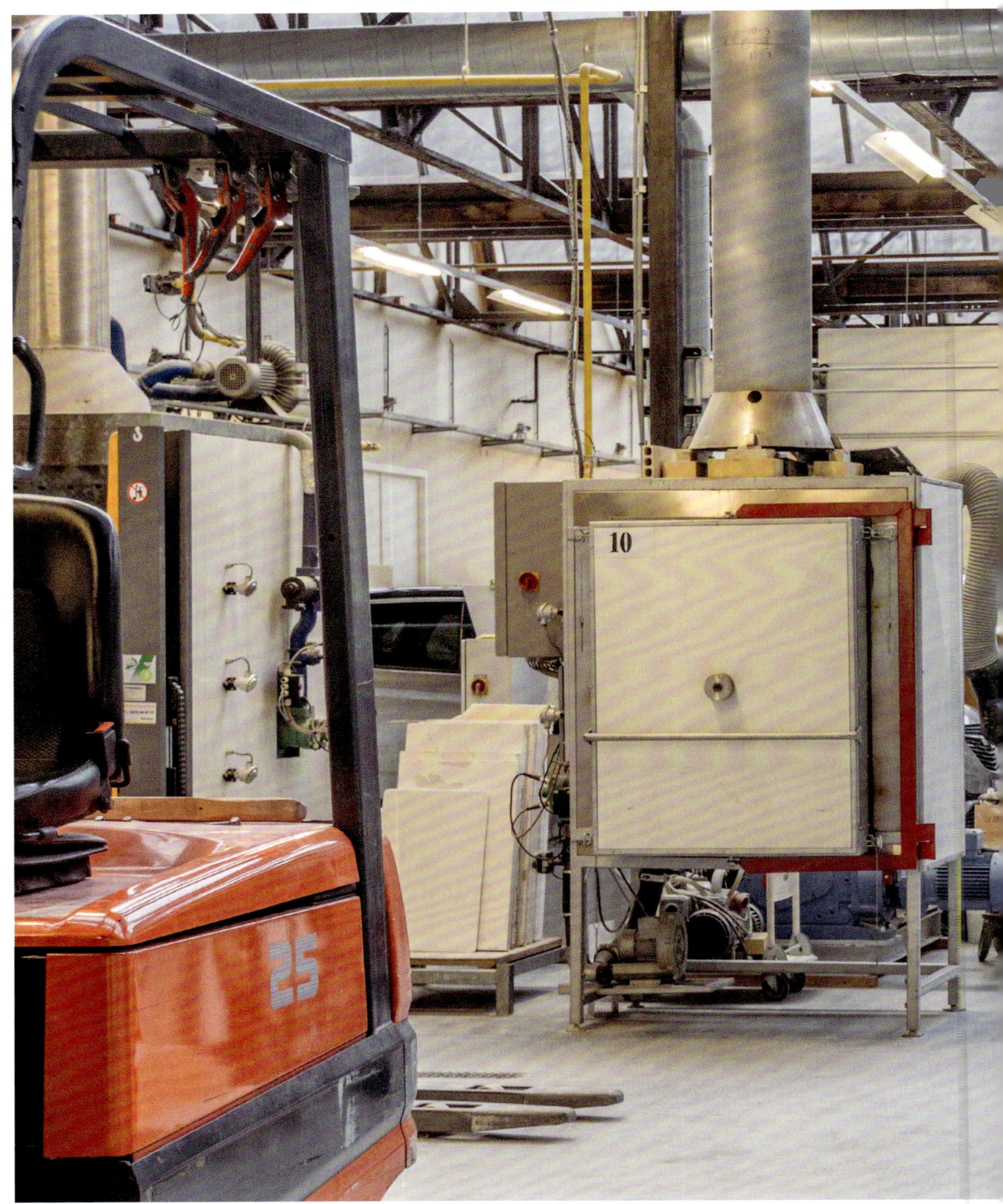

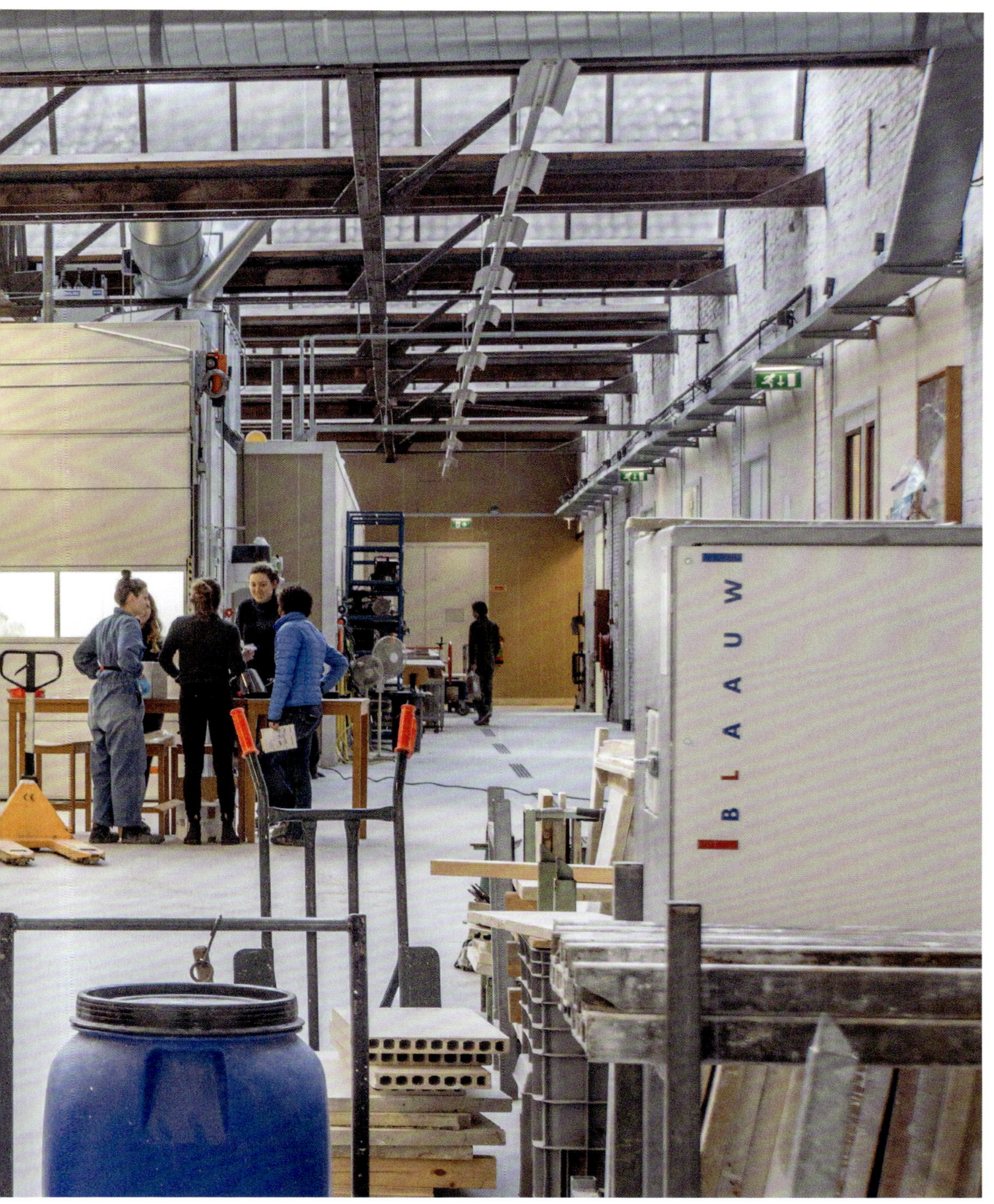

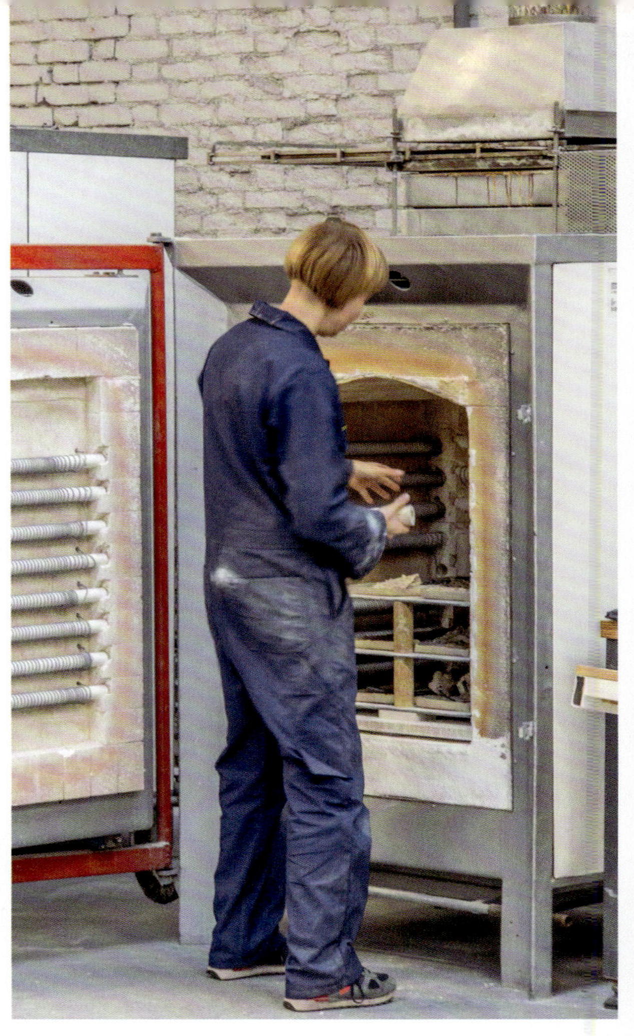

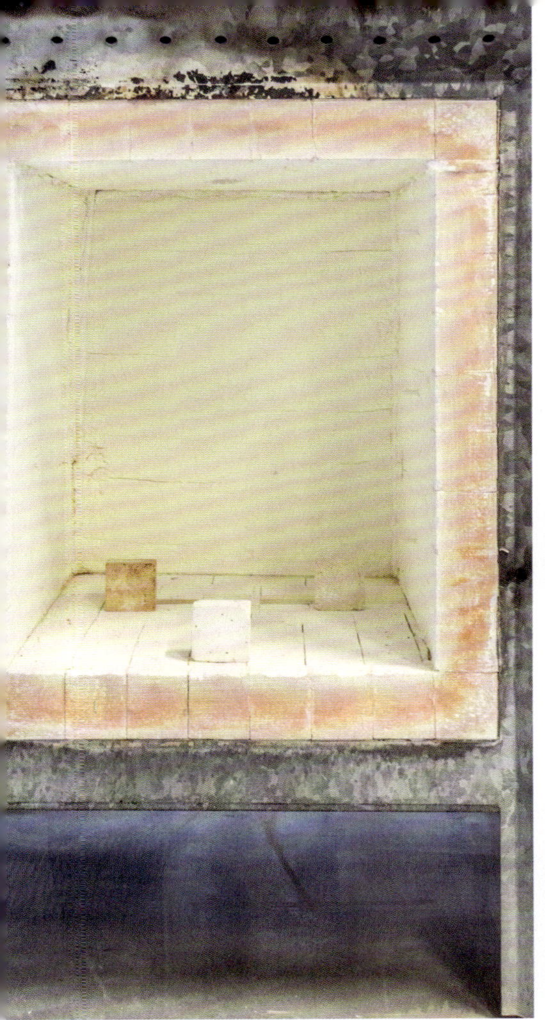
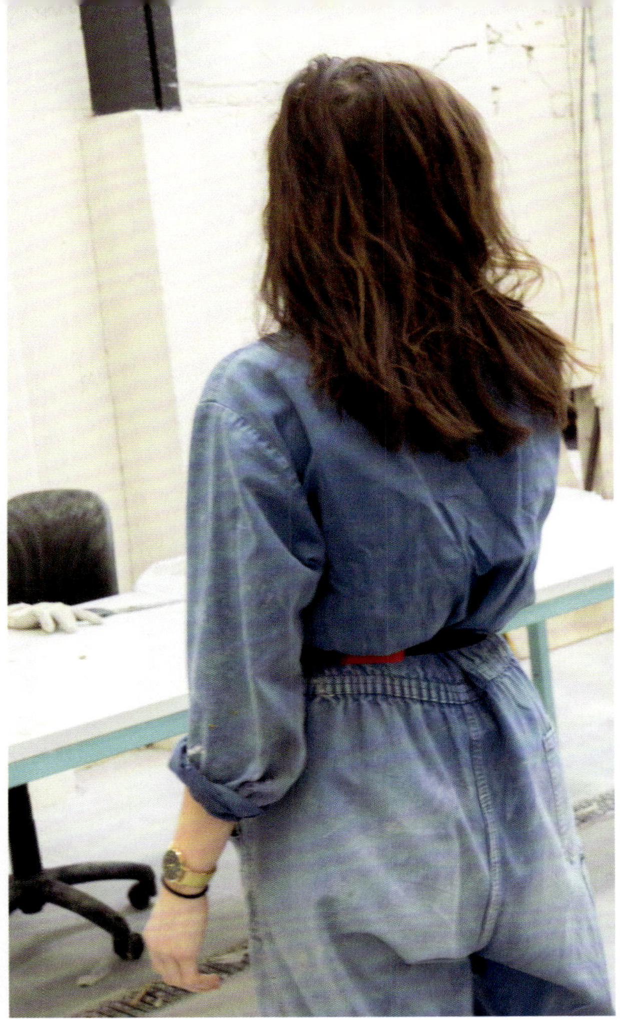

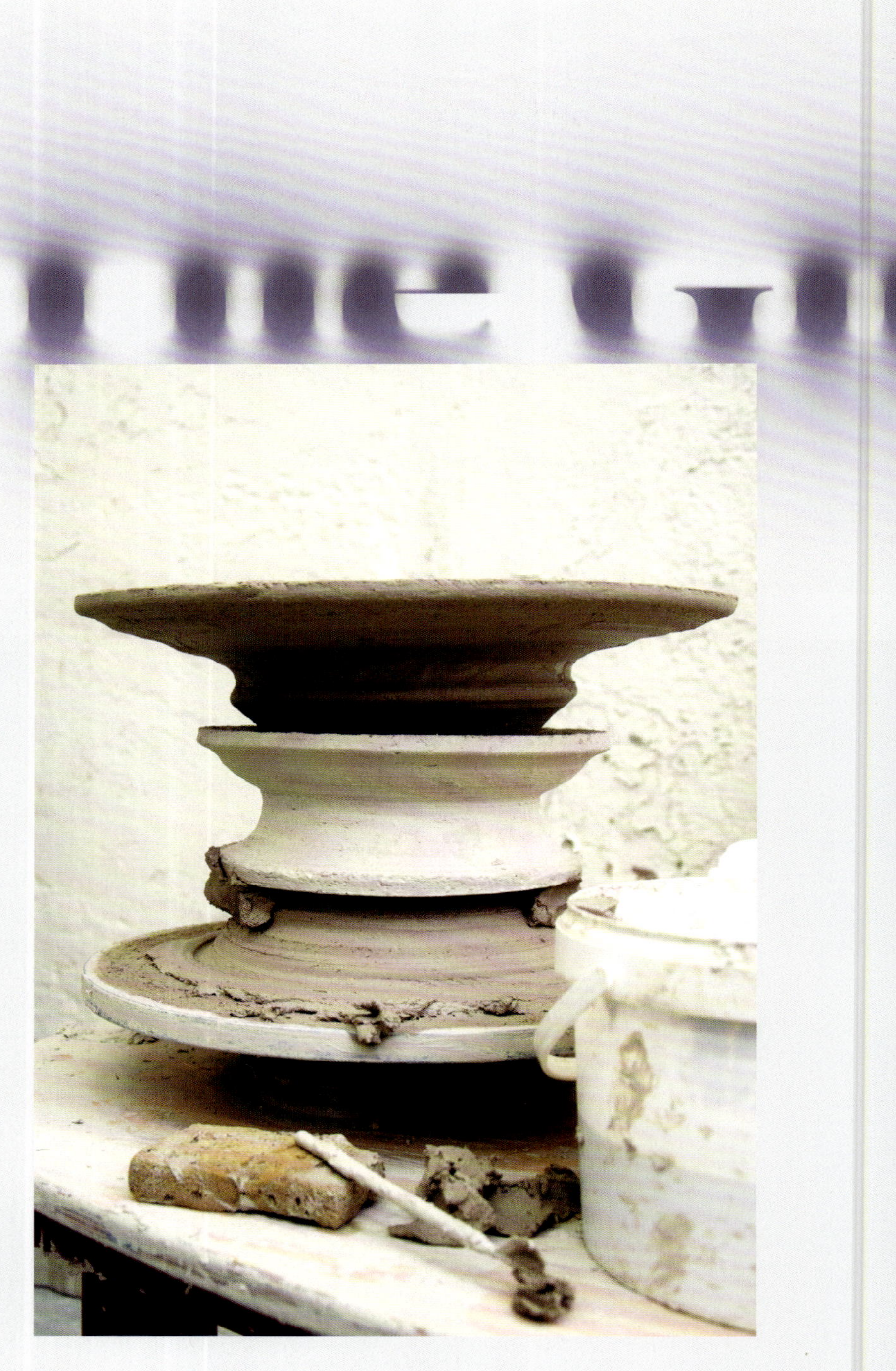

Timeline
50 years EKWC

1969

Establishment of Keramiek Werkcentrum (KWC) Heusden, postal address at Museum Boijmans Van Beuningen, Rotterdam. From the Memorandum of Association: 'Promoting the integration of the artist and his art in social life by opening a research and experimental ceramic work centre for the entire art world. Means: make available a modern well-equipped ceramics workspace; perform public relations work; make living and living space available.'

1970

Subsidies are received from the Ministry of Public Works, the Heusden Municipality and the province of North Brabant for the purchase and restoration of three monumental townhouses in Heusden.

1971

Opening of exhibition ceramics collection KWC, organized in Commiezenhuis, Heusden.

1973

Official opening of the KWC Heusden by Mr. J. Willems, representative of the province of North Brabant.

1979   1980   1983   1986

1979

Short note about the future of the KWC: 'Taking on developments' by Marja Hooft, Elly van den Bomen and Theo Laurentius.

Concept by Director Hans van Wijck for new setup of symposiums: 'We're not looking for ceramicists with a holy awe for the material and hysterical ideas about economical firing or going back to nature. We will be inviting people with innovative ideas and qualities. Who speak out and do not shy away from technical and aesthetic challenges that are clever. The emphasis is on ground-breaking and art-innovative principles.'

1980

Exhibition Jan Oosterman, founder of the KWC. First venue: KWC Heusden; second venue: Museum Princessehof, Leeuwarden.

1983

Exhibition on the occasion of ten years of participants in the KWC in Heusden. First venue: Kultureel Sentrum Tilburg; second venue: Stedelijk Museum Schiedam; third venue: Museum Waterland, Purmerend. Between 1973 and 1983, 120 participants completed a work period at the KWC.

1986

'Heusden (the Netherlands) meets Heusden (Belgium)'; work from the KWC meets work by painters from Heusden, Belgium.

1991

Relocation from Heusden to Den Bosch. New name: Europees Keramisch Werkcentrum (EKWC), European Ceramic Work Centre. The new premises measure 2000 m2 and host 12 artists studios and 12 apartments.

1992

Official opening of the new location on Zuid Willemsvaart 215, Den Bosch, by Minister Hedy d'Ancona.

Queen Beatrix visits the EKWC.

1999

'Idea on the Table': Dutch designers experiment with functional objects made of porcelain.

2003

'Dutch Souvenirs': 42 artists design a new type of souvenir, resulting in presentations at the Salone del Mobile, Milan and Galerie Binnen, Amsterdam.

2004

'Brick' and 'Combined residencies': introduction of architecture at the EKWC.

Purchase of a digital milling machine.

International project with China: 'Dutch-Chinese Ceramic Project', resulting in presentations in SM's Stedelijk Museum Den Bosch (2005) and Central Academy of Fine Arts in Beijing (2006).

2005

Publication *The Ceramic Process*. The fourth edition was published in 2017, followed by a Chinese translation in 2019.

International project with Senegal: 'Boumbaclaque', resulting in presentations in Museum Princessehof Leeuwarden (2005) and during the Biennale Dak'Art in Dakar (2006).

Presentation of the Dutch Ceramics Award by the Den Bosch Ceramics City Foundation, a collaboration of the EKWC, the Stedelijk Museum Den Bosch, Cor Unum and the Academy for Art and Design/St. Joost.

2006

Wienerberger BV becomes the centre's main sponsor (until 2011).

International project with Morocco: 'Ceramic Ideas', resulting in a presentation at gallery Majke Hüsstege, Den Bosch.

2009

'Ceramics & Architecture' for Dutch Design Week Eindhoven, Klokgebouw. EKWC will also present design and ceramics at the Dutch Design Weeks 2011, 2012 and 2013, often in collaboration with Beeldenstorm Eindhoven, Glasmuseum Leerdam and AGA Amsterdam.

2010

Opening of fablab, made possible by a European Union grant.

2011

Presentation 'EKWC' during the British Ceramic Biennale.

Presentation 'Sound & Ceramics' and 'Cadcam', Ceramics Biennale Korea (GICB).

Introduction of the name Sundaymorning@ EKWC.

2012

Prinsjesdag
The government decides to stop the subsidy for the period 2013-2016. Participants must acquire their own resources, with the generous support of the Mondriaan Fund.

2013

Start of the collaboration with Saga Ceramic Research Laboratory, Japan. Resulting in two symposiums in Arita (2016) and Museum Princessehof Leeuwarden (2018).

2015

Move from Den Bosch to Oisterwijk. The Oisterwijk venue offers 5,000 m2, including 16 studio's, 17 guestrooms, two galleries for visitors to see the results of the residencies and space to engage in student projects. Fontys Tilburg, HKU Utrecht, Design Academy Eindhoven and St. Lucas Boxtel regularly use the facilities.

2016

Official opening of the Almystraat 10 building, Oisterwijk, by Minister Jet Bussemaker.

The minister grants the Centre a four-year subsidy. Sundaymorning@ EKWC is the only institute in the Netherlands to not receive subsidy in 2013 and then, one term later, to receive funds from the Cultural Basic Infrastructure of the state.

2017

Start of collaboration with the eight most important ceramics residencies in China, Japan, Korea, Taiwan and England. Exchange of participants and staff members.

Province of North Brabant includes the centre in the Basic Infrastructure of the province.

Publication of Nick Renshaw's book: *DEMYSTIFIED The European Ceramic Workcentre as Centre of Excellence*

Exhibition 'Urnen', with GICB, Korea.

2018

'Cool Ceramic Hunt': international trend research by Carl Rohde on the development of tableware. Commissioned by Sundaymorning@ EKWC.

2019

Sundaymorning@
EKWC acquires the
building in Oisterwijk
from the province of
North Brabant.

Start of jubilee year
2019, to commemorate
Sundaymorning@
EKWC's fiftieth anni-
versary with exhibitions
in Den Bosch, The
Hague, Amsterdam,
Heusden and Tilburg, a
residency programme
in Jingdezhen, China,
and a traveling
exhibition in China.
Opening of EKWC
store in Jingdezhen.

'Ghosts of Sunday
Morning': exhibition in
Design Museum
Den Bosch on the
occasion of 50 years
EKWC.

Directors

1973 - 1975	Phillip Gearheart
1976 - 1988	Hans van Wijck
1987 - 1998	Adriaan van Spanje (general director)
1990 - 1999	Xavier Toubes (artistic director)
1998 - 1999	Joop van Wingarden (interim director)
1999 - 2009	Koos de Jong
From 2010	Ranti Tjan

Board

1969

W. Kramer
B.R.M. de Neeve
C. Lith
Jan Oosterman
Jan van de Vaart

1971

W. Kramer
B.R.M. de Neeve
A.J.A. van Dijk
W.A.J. Hansen
J.J. Oosterman
B. Premsela
J.J. van der Vaart
S. Valkema

1979

Th. Laurentius
M. van Eeden-Douglas
A. de Jong
E. van den Bomen
B. de Neeve
M. Hooft
J. Mobach
M. Kuijpers
H. Severijns
L. Tegenbosch
J. van Berkom
P. Hagenaars
H. Koopmans
H. Verberkmoes
H. Mooy
M. Mager
T. van der Rotten

1982

Wim Korink
Anton Reijnders
Maaike Thijssen
Anco Hermans
Corien Ridderikhoff
Mees van den Eeden
Ton van der Rotten
Lambert Tegenbosch
Adri de Jong
Hein Severijns

1986

Wim Korink
Hans Jurgens
Toos de Klerk
Eric Ebbinge
Ardje de Graaf
Hein Severijns
Abel te Velde
Henriette Verburgh

1988

H.A. Kossman
P. Schwartz
G.P. Stips-van Weel
H. Jurgens
H. Mobach

1997

J.L.P. Post
L. Brandt Corstius
C.J. de Jager
H.A. Kossmann
H. Oestreicher
J. Smits
A.H.G.M. Voogt

2007

Bianca de Poorter
Lydie Donner
Paul Mertz
Abel Cahen
Norman Trapman

2011

Ilja van Haren
Amo Bosman
Aart Wijnen
Simone van Bakel
Marien Schouten
Ernst van Alphen
Hans van Duijn

2015

Hans van Duijn
Ad van Berlo
Aart Wijnen
Simone van Bakel
Marien Schouten
Ernst van Alphen
Amo Bosman

2019

Irene Fortuyn
Anne Wenzel
Thomas Eyck
Amo Bosman

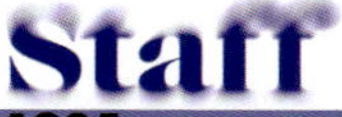 Staff

1985

H. van Wijck, workshop coordinator

M. van den Eeden-Douglas, staff member

D. Sandrock-Gille, library and documentation

M. Spruit -Ledeboer, library and documentation

1988

Adriaan van Spanje, director

Anton Reijnders, workshop supervisor

Leon van der Werff, assistant workshop coordina-

tor, concierge

Helen van Delft, staff member, librarian

Yvette Lardinois, office

Susie van der Aalst, office assistant

1998

Adriaan van Spanje, general director

Xavier Toubes, artistic director

Henk Geel, workshop metal & wood

Will van Hassel, workshop assistant

Matthias Keller, workshop supervisor moulds

Mark Kohlen, workshop moulds

Peter Oltheten, workshop supervisor

Ine Peels, workshop

Anton Reijnders, workshop coordinator

Bo Ruimers, workshop, kiln master

Han Sietsma, workshop, glazes

Andrea Wach, workshop assistant glazes

Yvette Lardinois, presentation officer

Jo Luitjes, custodian

Lianne van Someren, secretary

Margreet van Uffelen, secretary

Wilma Fraaij, secretary

Yvonne Lapre, secretary

Helma van Boxtel, housekeeping

Anne Brands, housekeeping

Staff

2007

Koos de Jong, director

Marc Graetz, corporate manager

Peter Oltheten, head workshop

Froukje van Baren, workshop, research

Marlies Crooijmans, workshop, repro

Marc Kohlen, workshop, mould making

Marianne Peijnenburg, workshop

Andrea Wach, workshop

Guido van Ophoven, workshop, transport and stock

Lydia Denters, instructor

Harry Koopman, instructor woodwork shop

Manon Jacobs, documentation and publicity

Noor Zwinkels, project leader and PR/communication

Wies van Opstal, office

Anouk Rooth, office

Betty Schollaert, secretary

Ageeth Iepema, secretary

Linda Barkhuijzen, housekeeping

Theo van den Oetelaar, housekeeping

Lidy van Koningsbrugge, housekeeping

2012

Ranti Tjan, director

Sander Alblas, advisor, digital techniques

Froukje van Baren, advisor, research

Guido Ophoven, transport and stock

Peter Oltheten, advisor, head workshop

Marianne Peijnenburg, advisor

Linda Barkhuijzen, housekeeping

Monique Ouwers, housekeeping

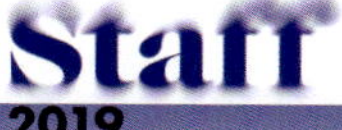

Staff

2019

Ranti Tjan, director

Sander Alblas, advisor, digital techniques

Froukje van Baren, advisor, research

Annette van den Hout, stock and transport

Katrin Konig, advisor

Nico Thone, coordinator internal and external affairs

Peter Oltheten, head workshop, advisor kilns

Marianne Peijnenburg, advisor

Pierluigi Pompei, advisor, moulds

Yves Brandsma, caretaker

Debby Lutter, assistant caretaker

Bianca van Baast, library

Annelies Broenink, coordinator tours

Esther Cuppen, documentation

Myra van Esch, education

Erwin Nijholt, administrator

Jeroen Rozema, coffee roaster

Jorg van Schijndel, coffee roaster

Leslie Segeren, housekeeping

Monique Ouwers, housekeeping

Linda Barkhuijzen, housekeeping

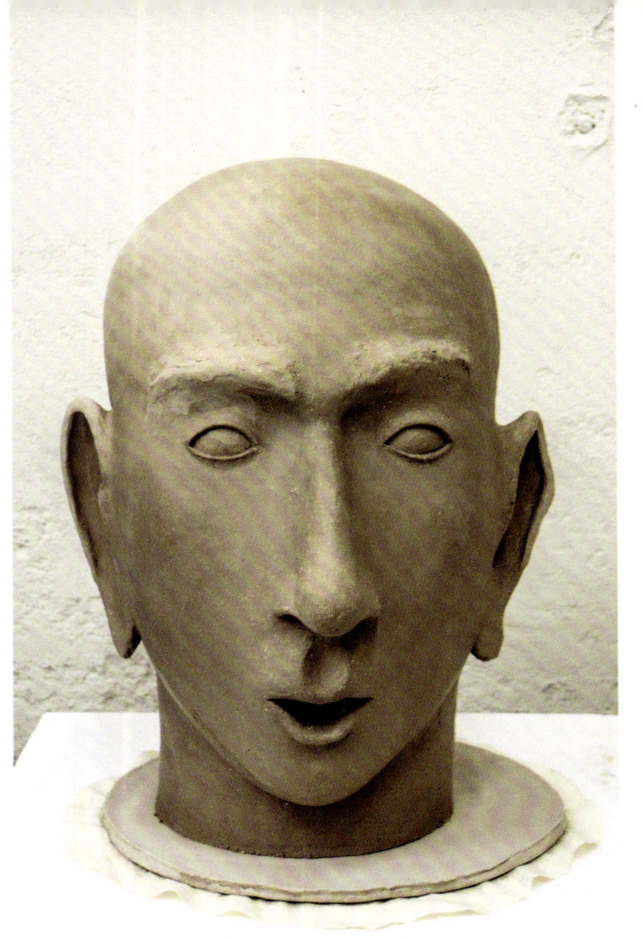

HARTMUT WILKENING, *WILLY CLAES*, 1999

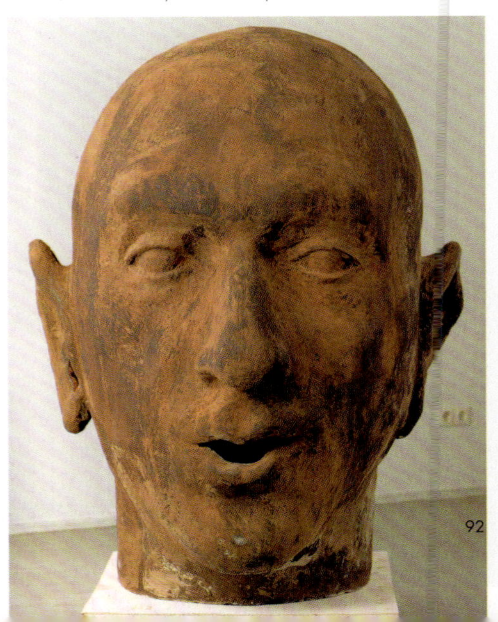

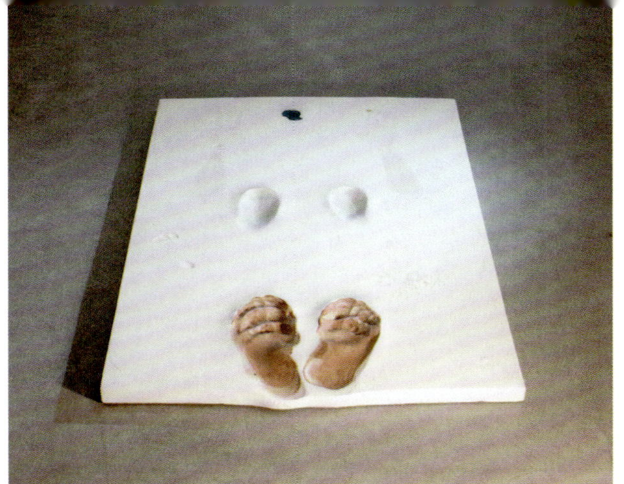

CANAN DAGDELEN, *UNTITLED*, 2001

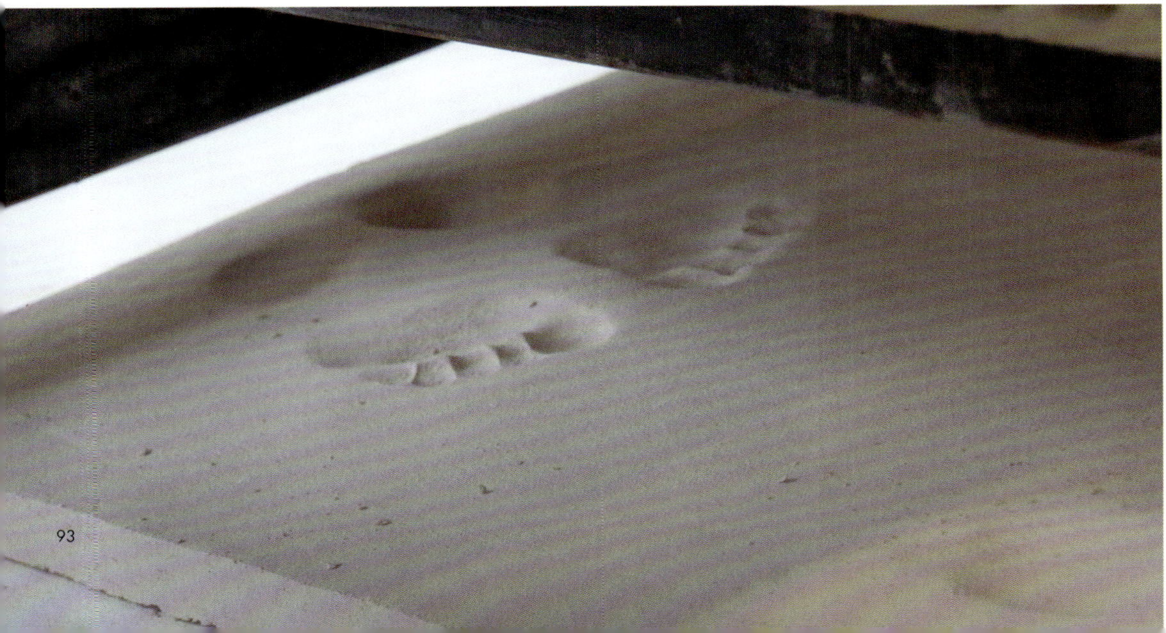

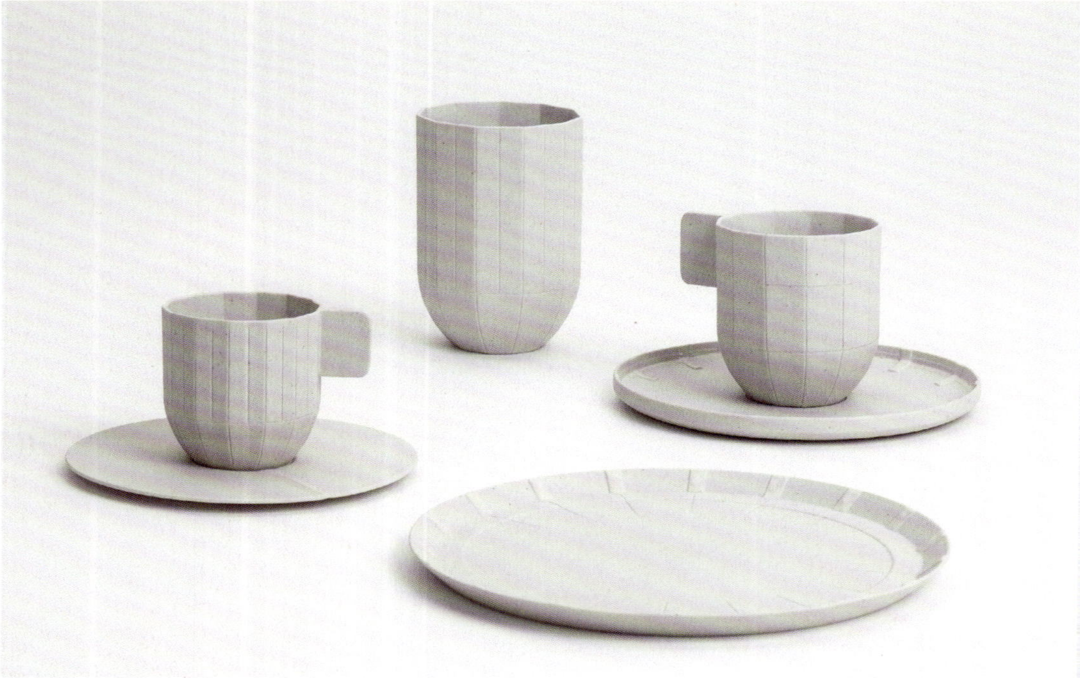

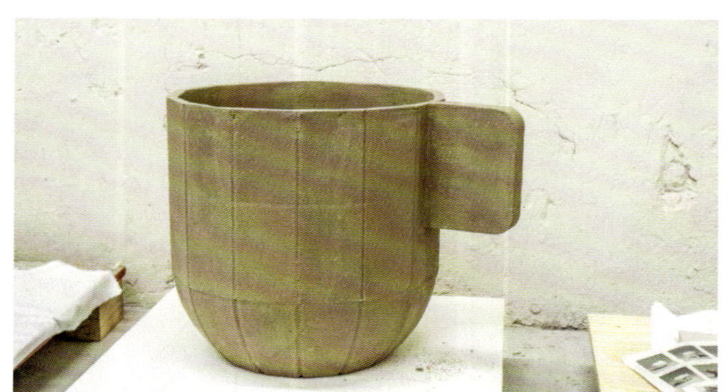

SCHOLTEN & BAIJINGS, *PAPER PORCELAIN*, 2009

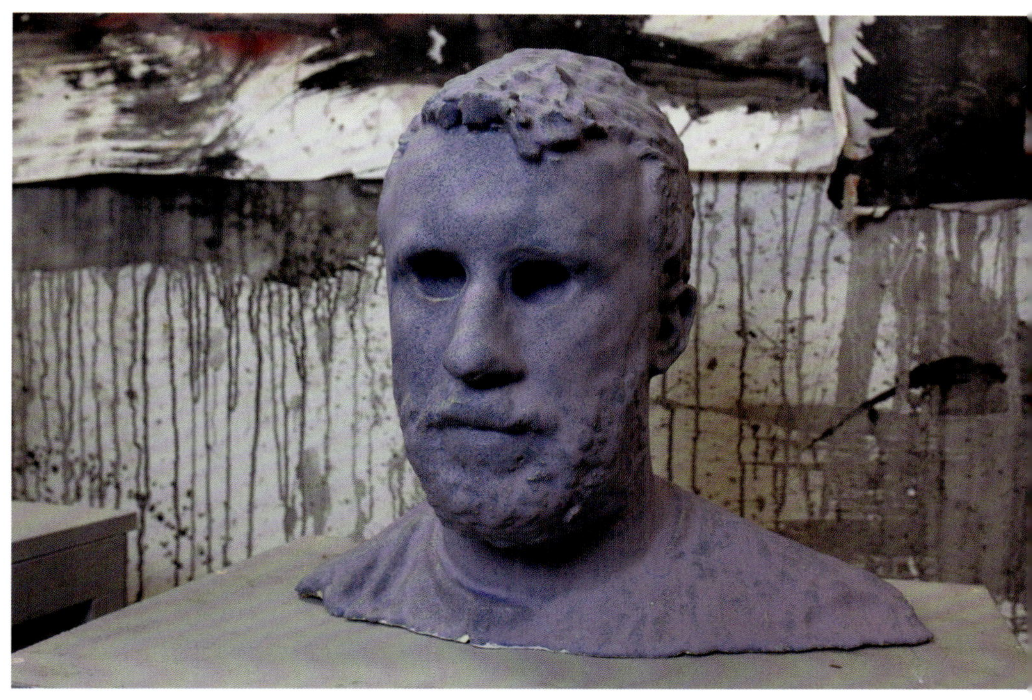

FRASER STEWART, *BLIND ACCEPTANCE*, 2017

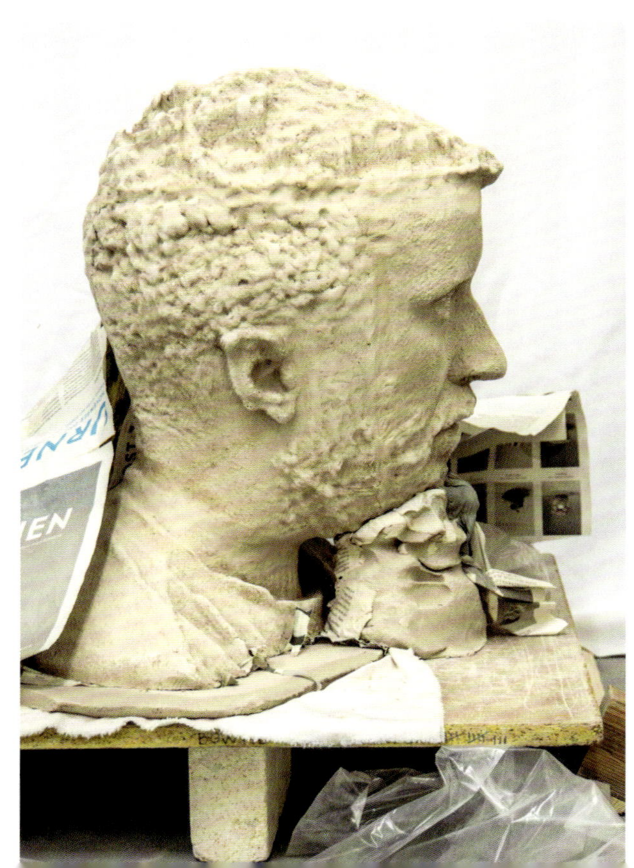

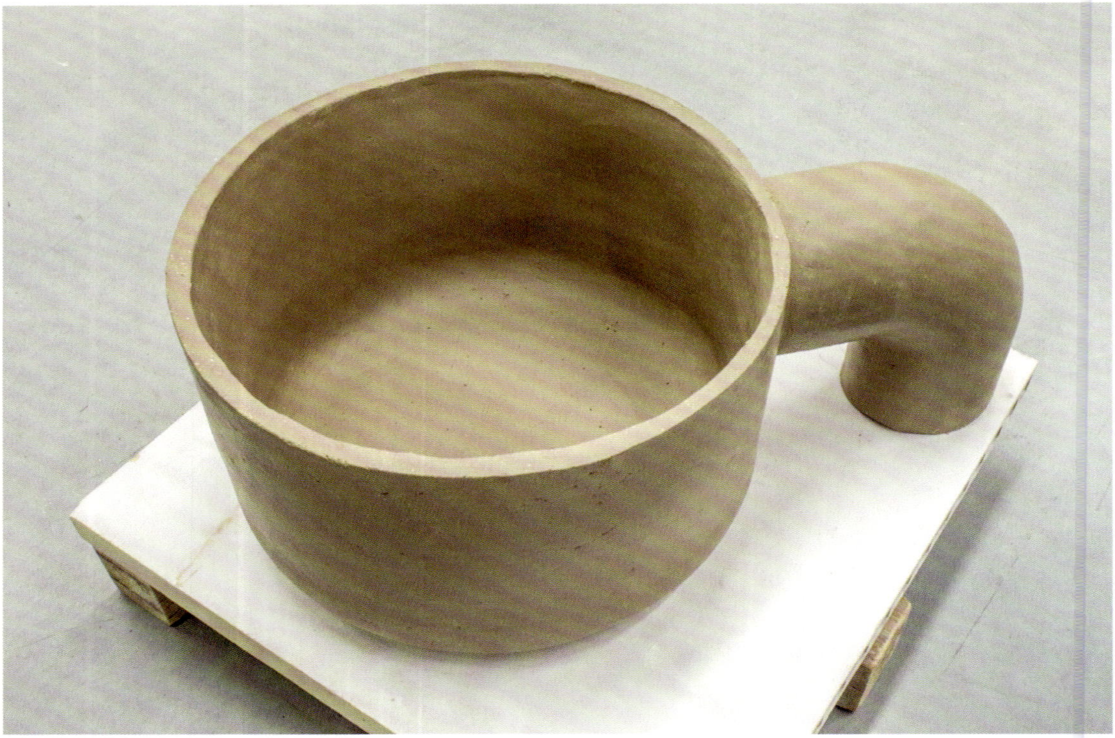

INEKE HANS, *BLACK GOLD*, 2002

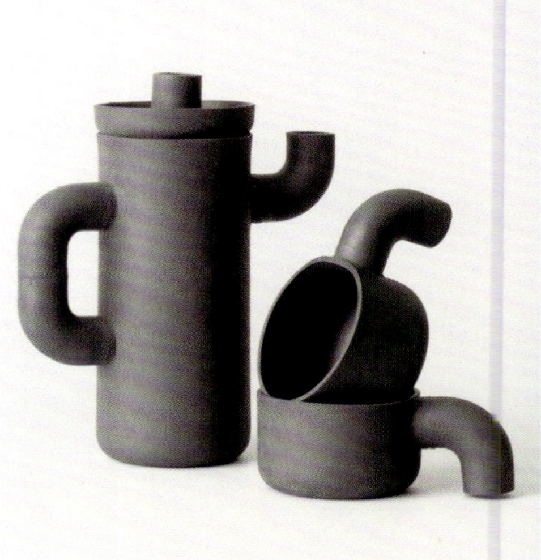

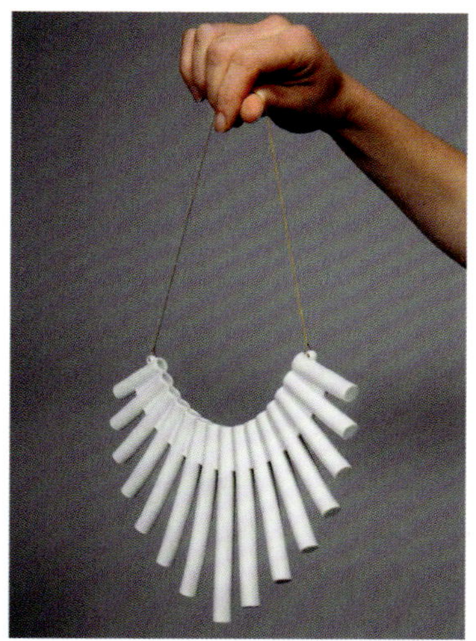

CHRISTIE WRIGHT AND ARJEN NOORDEMAN,
AUDIOWEAR, 2010

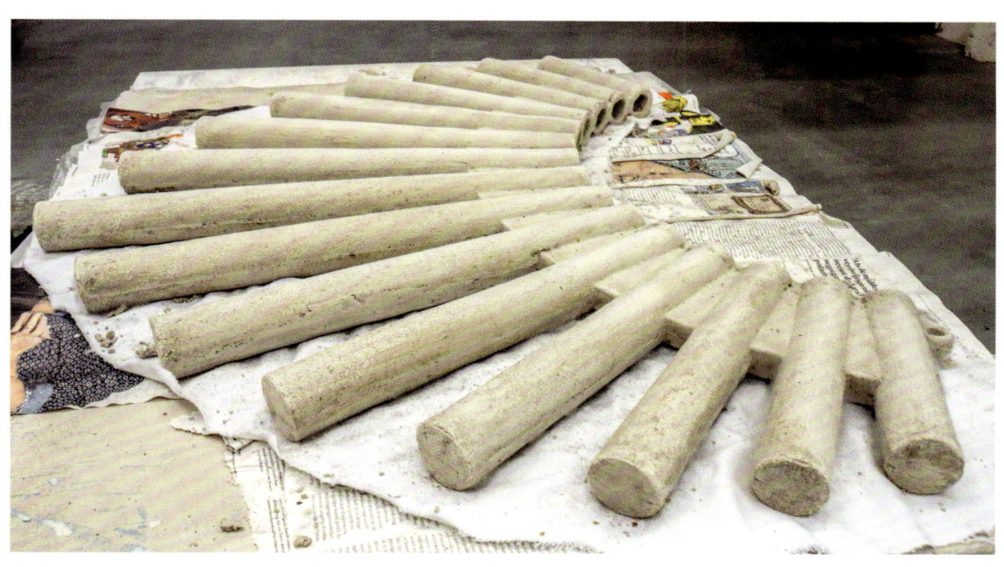

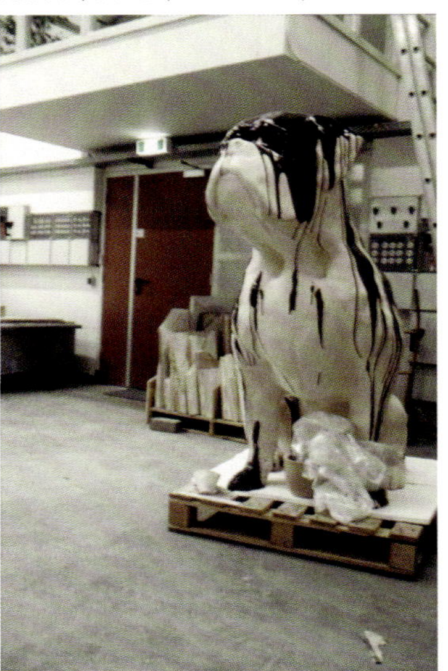

FORTUYN/O'BRIEN, *CAVE CANEM*, 1993

ANISH KAPOOR, *UNTITLED*, 1994

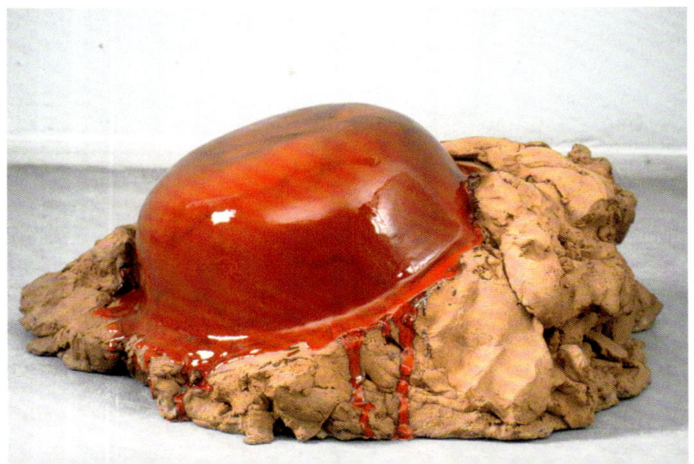

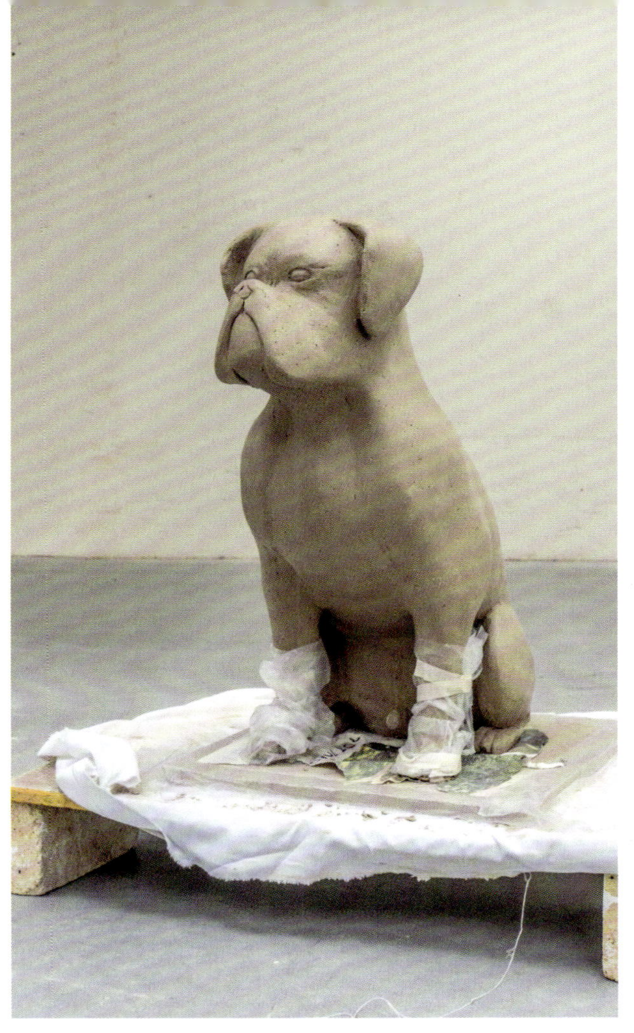

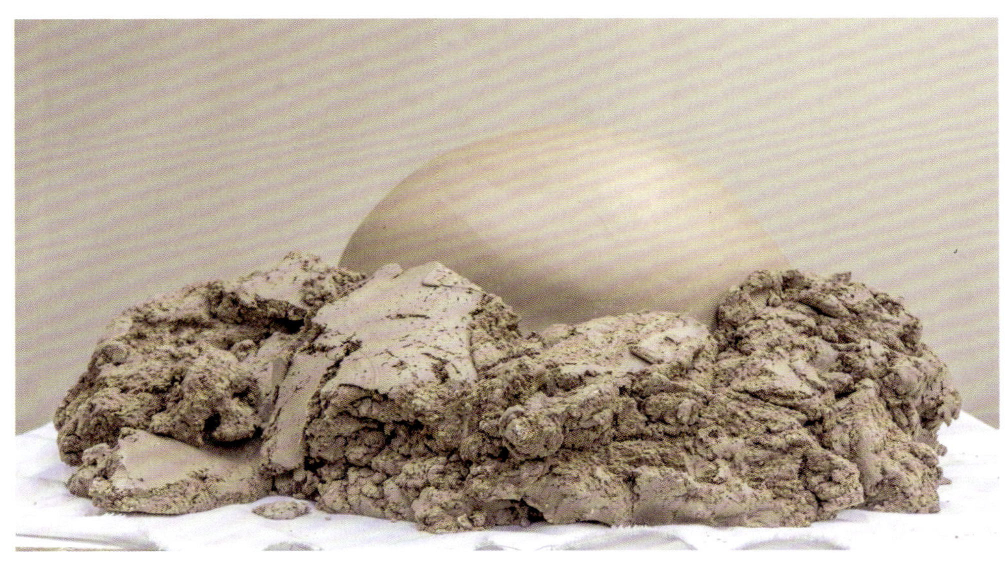

COUZIJN VAN LEEUWEN, *SEPARATED VASE*, 2005

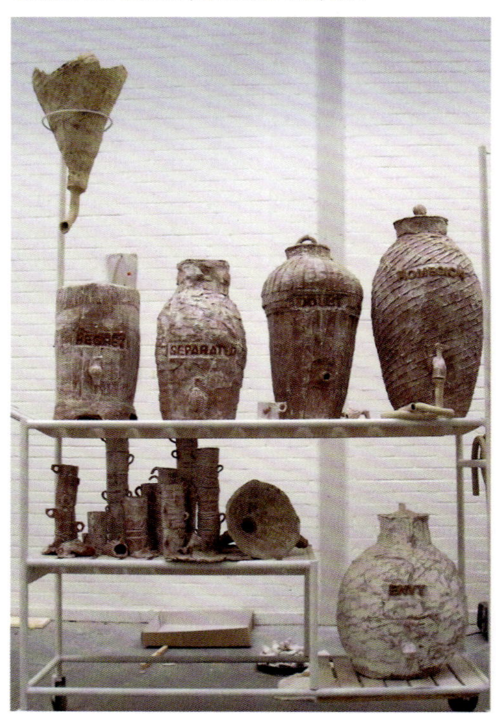

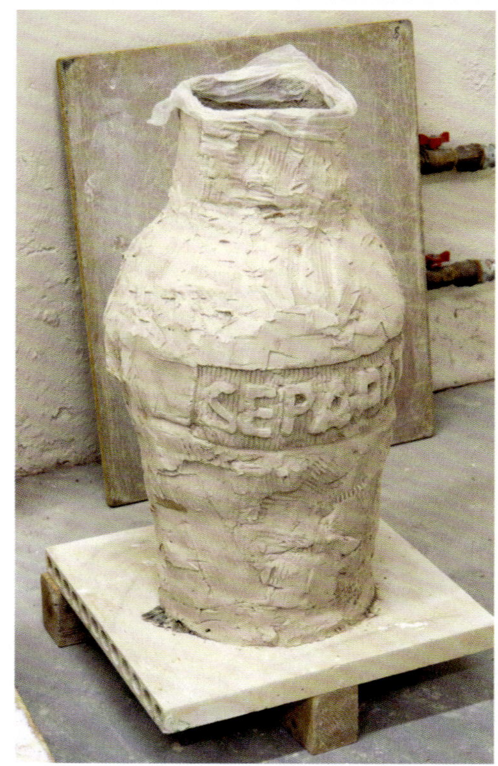

GIJS ASSMANN, *MY DEAR*, 1997

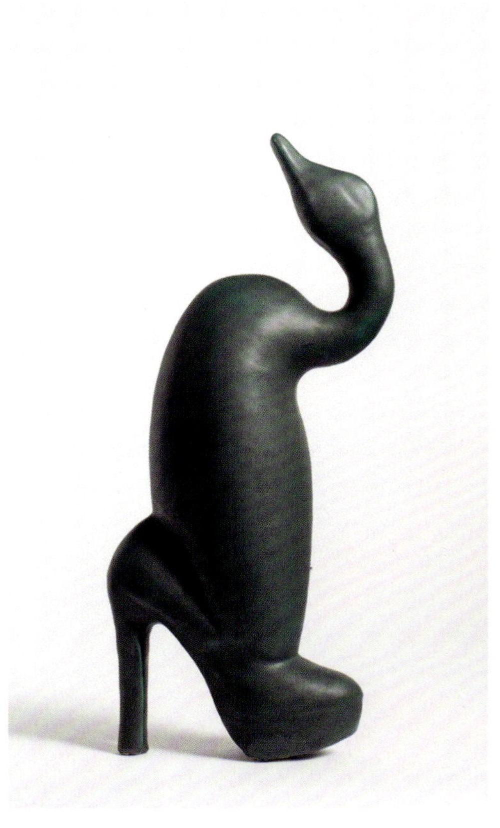

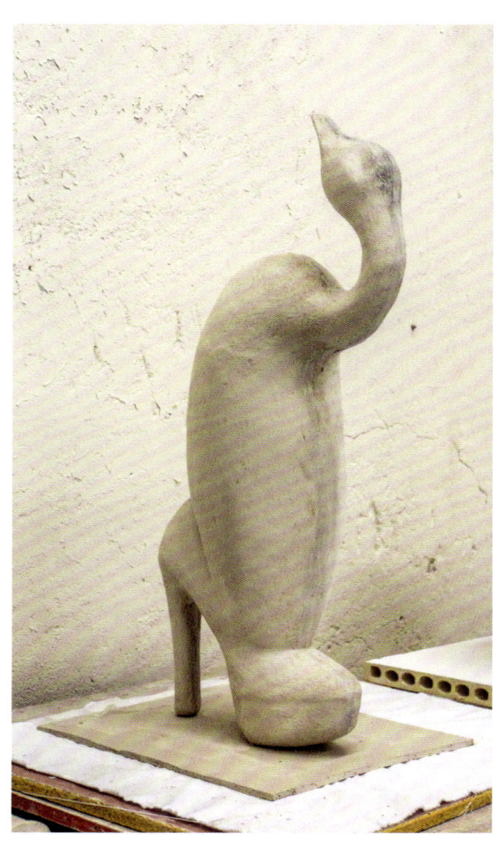

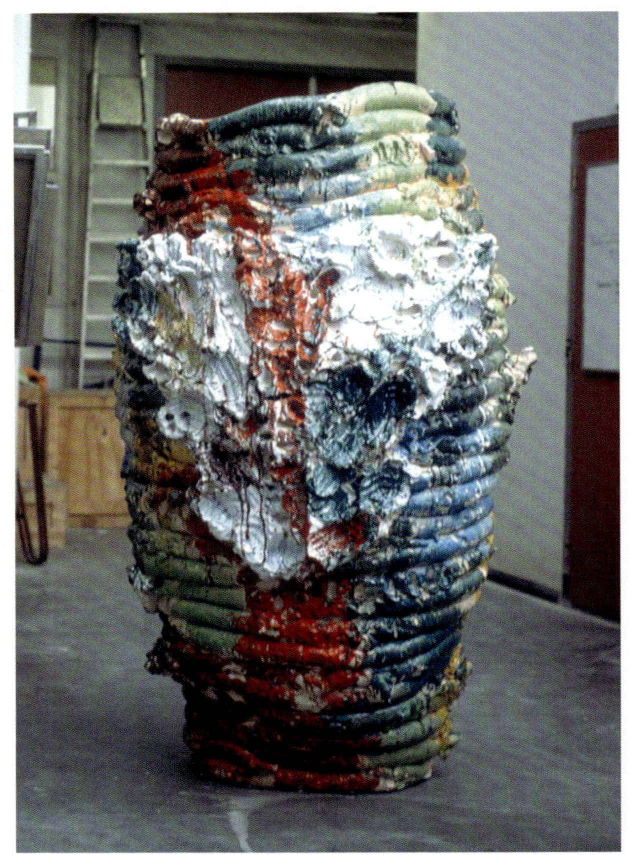

NORBERT PRANGENBERG, *FIGUR (1998)*, 1998

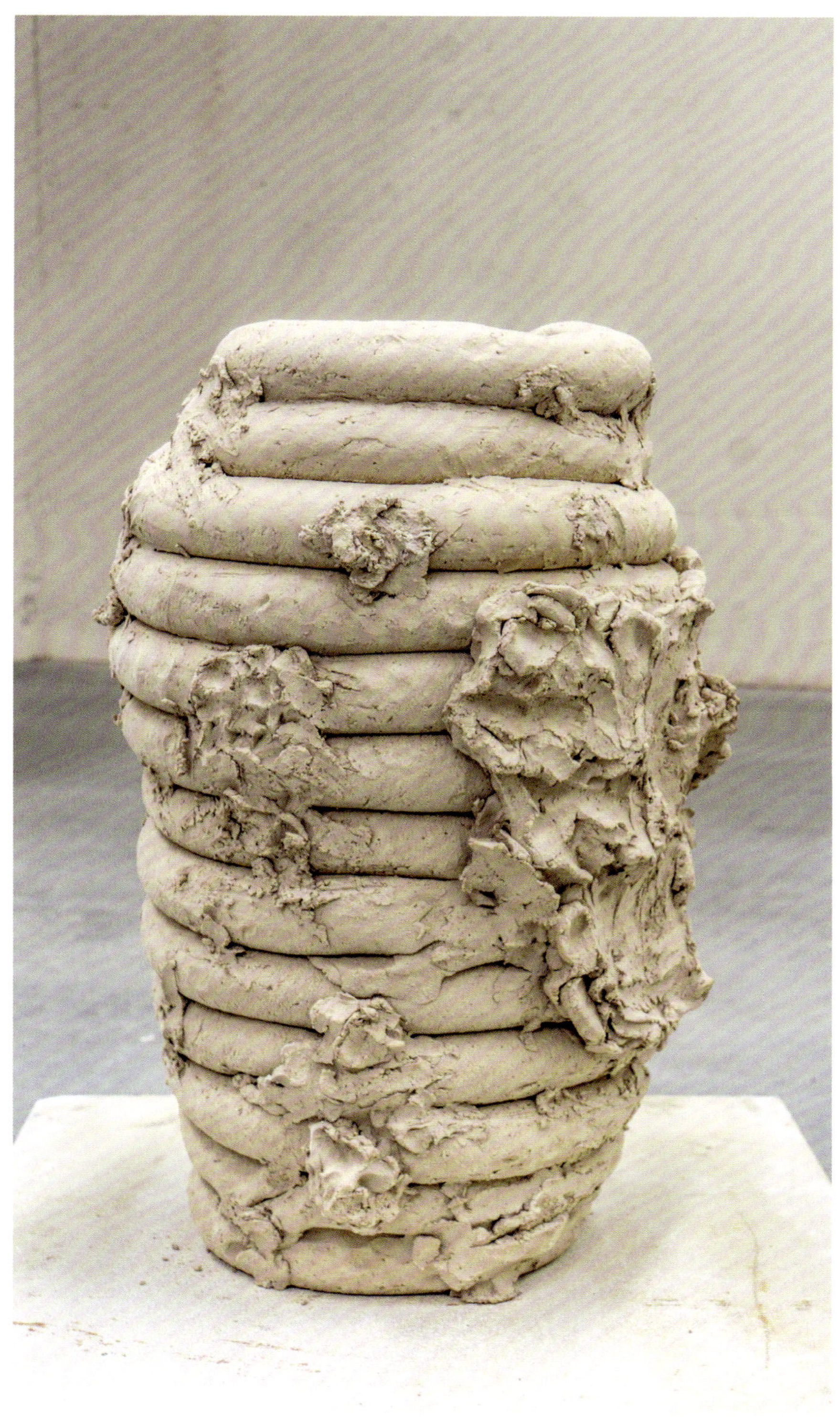

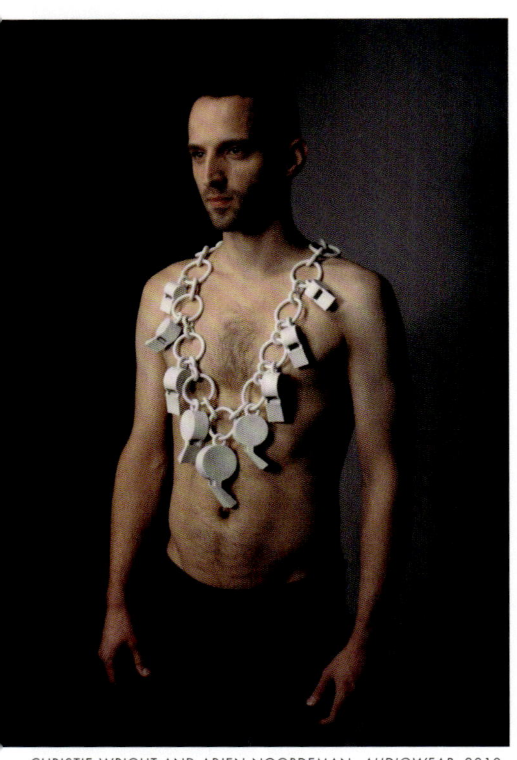

CHRISTIE WRIGHT AND ARJEN NOORDEMAN, *AUDIOWEAR*, 2010

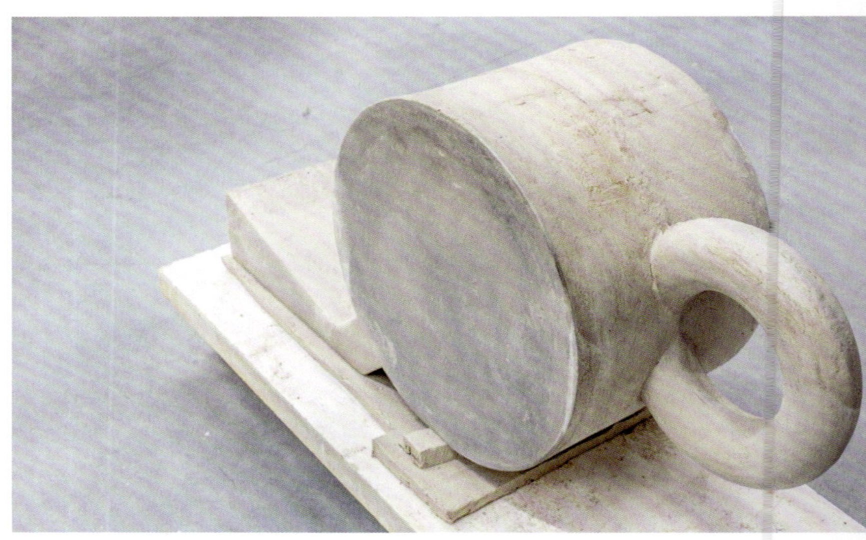

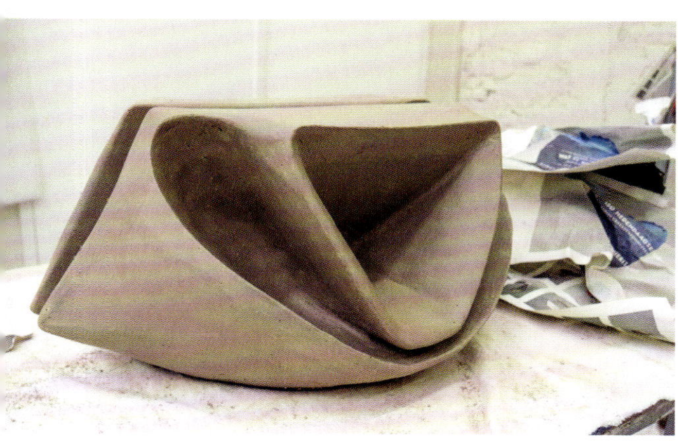

KATRIN MUELLER RUSSO AND RHETT RUSSO, *T-STOOL*, 2012

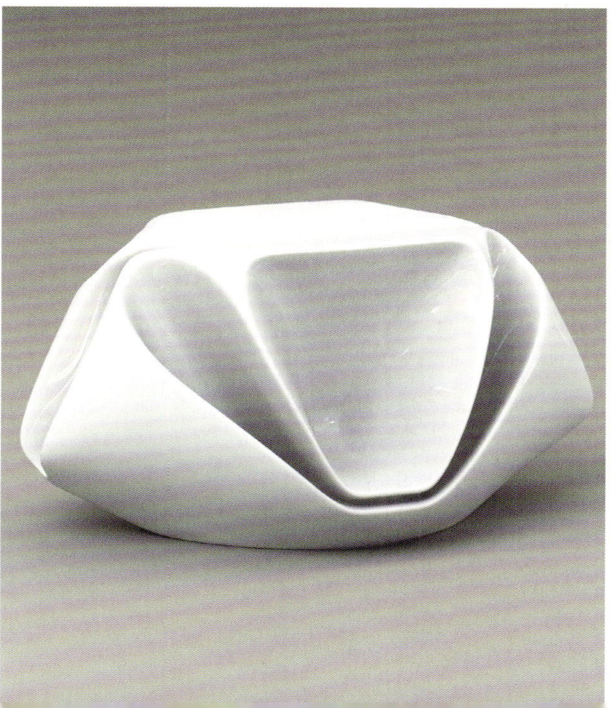

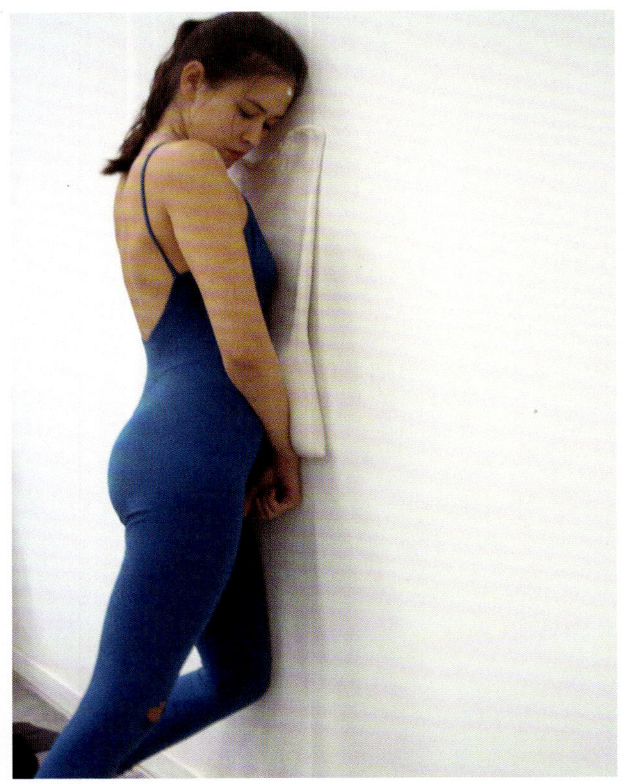

STEPHANIE DAVIDSON AND KATIE EWALD, *BODY-IMPRINTED TILES*, 2007

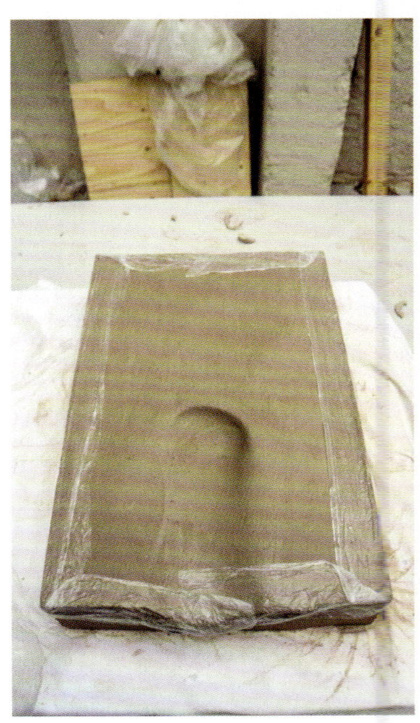

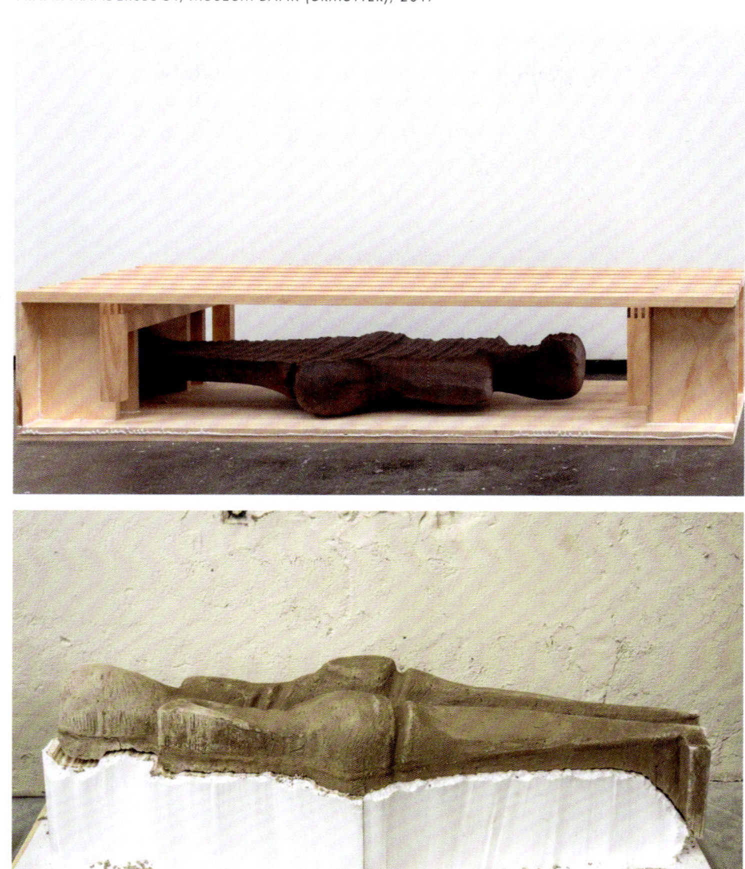

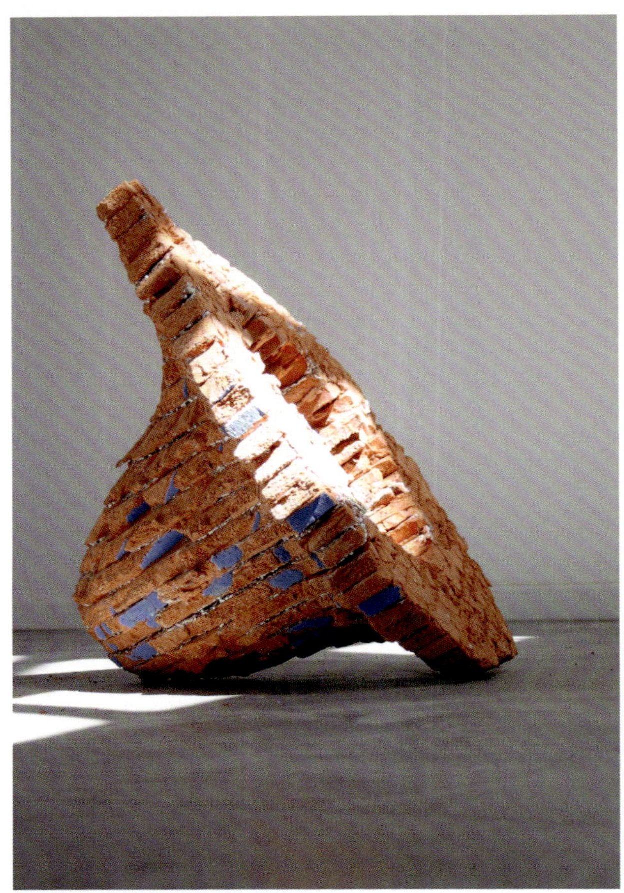

ANDREW BURTON, *BRICK WORKS*, 2007

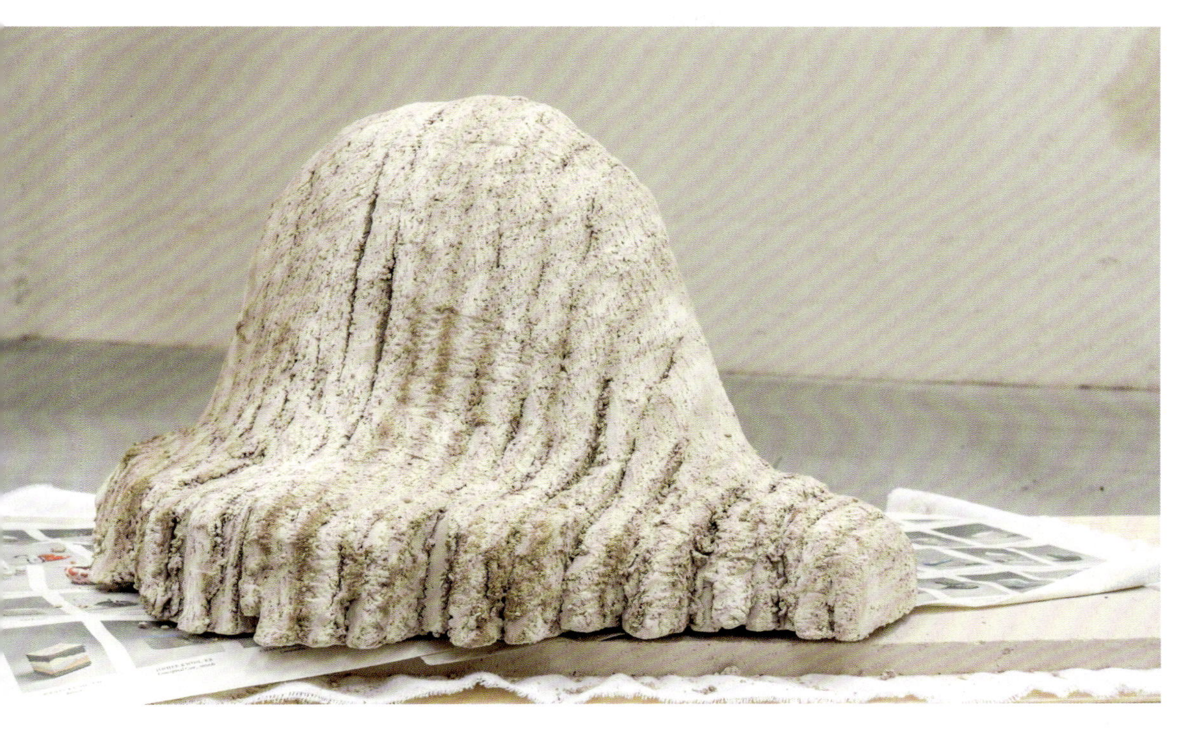

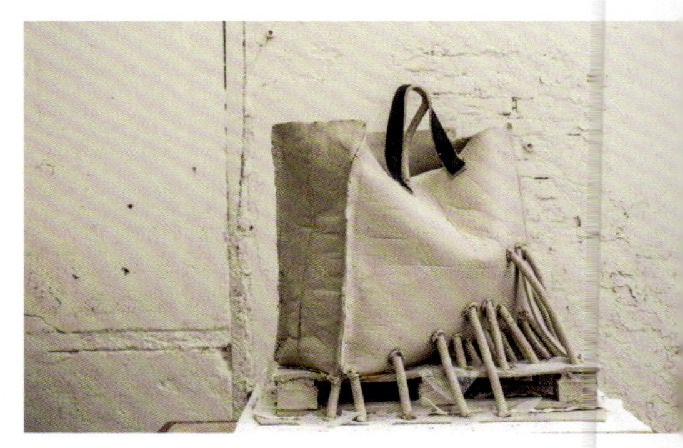

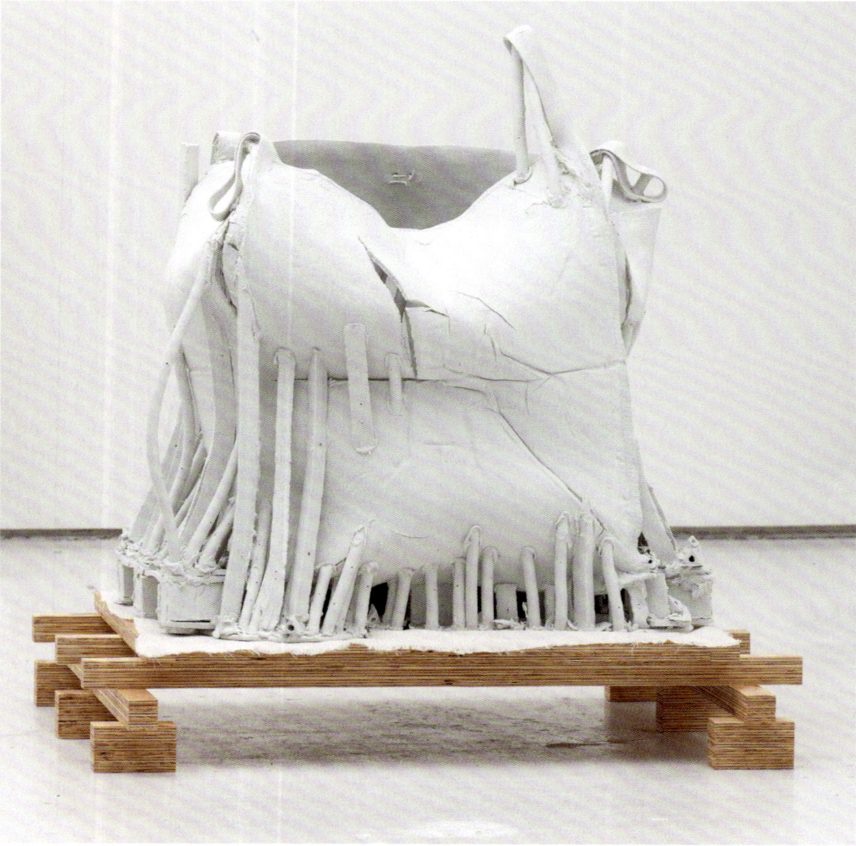

TIM BREUKERS, *BIG BAG*, 2011

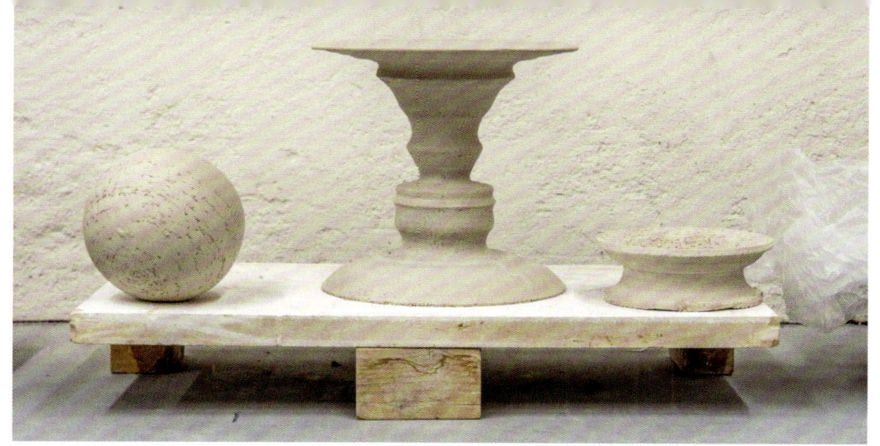

ANDREW LORD, *PROFILE VASE (PICASSO), 'ATLAS OF THE WORLD' AND STRETCHED VAN DER LECK*, 2002
COURTESY THE ARTIST AND GLADSTONE GALLERY, NEW YORK AND BRUSSELS

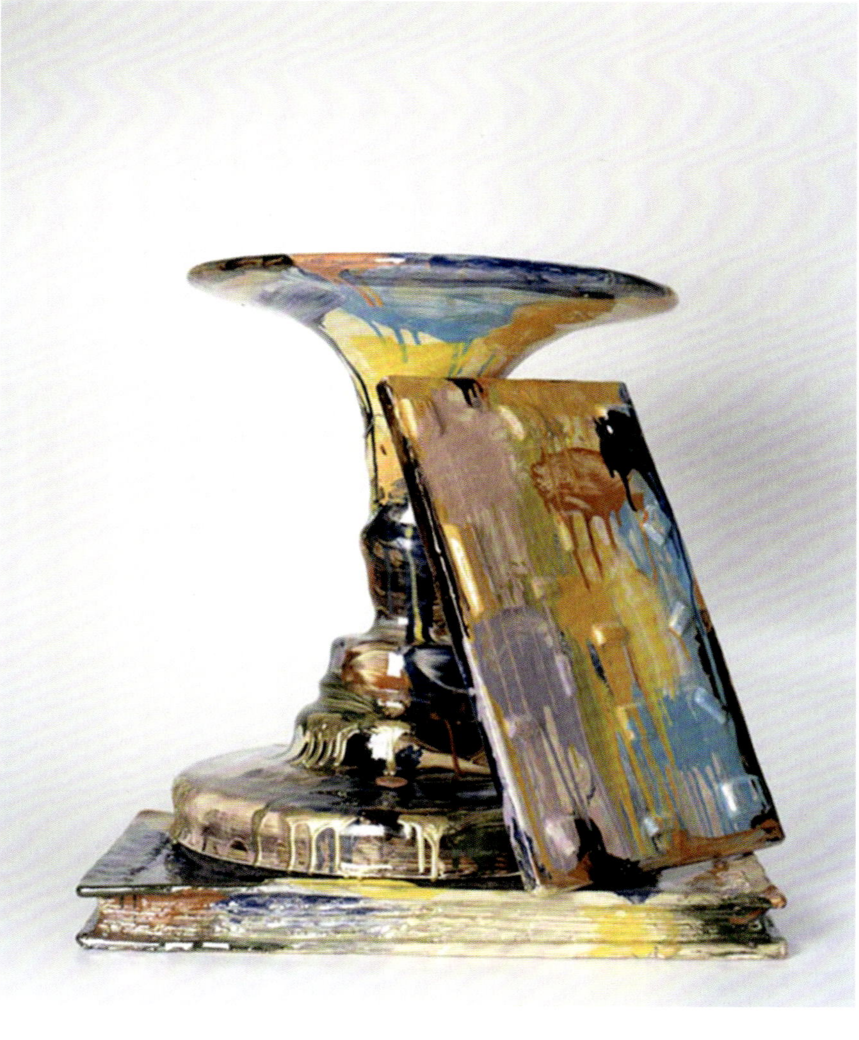

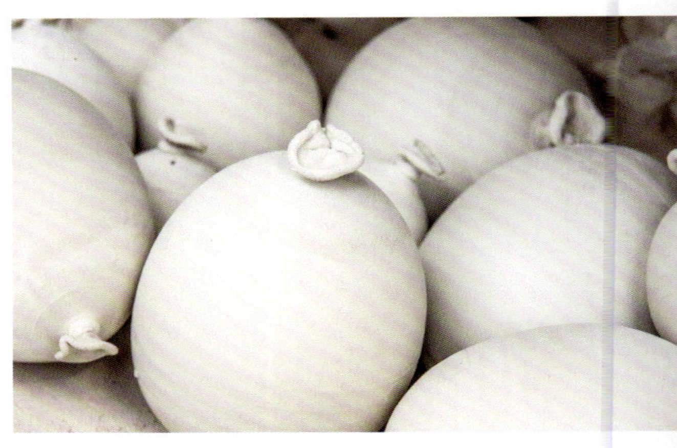

GABRIELLE WAMBAUGH, *MARVELLOUS MARIA MAGDALENA IN THE CLOUDS*, 2015

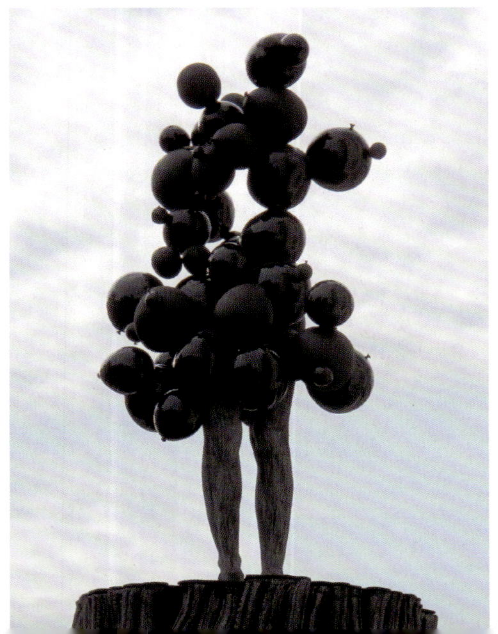

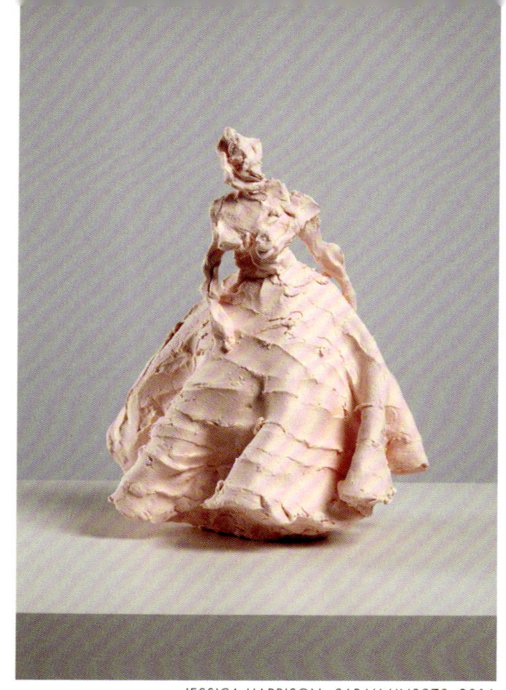

JESSICA HARRISON, *SARAH HN3978*, 2016

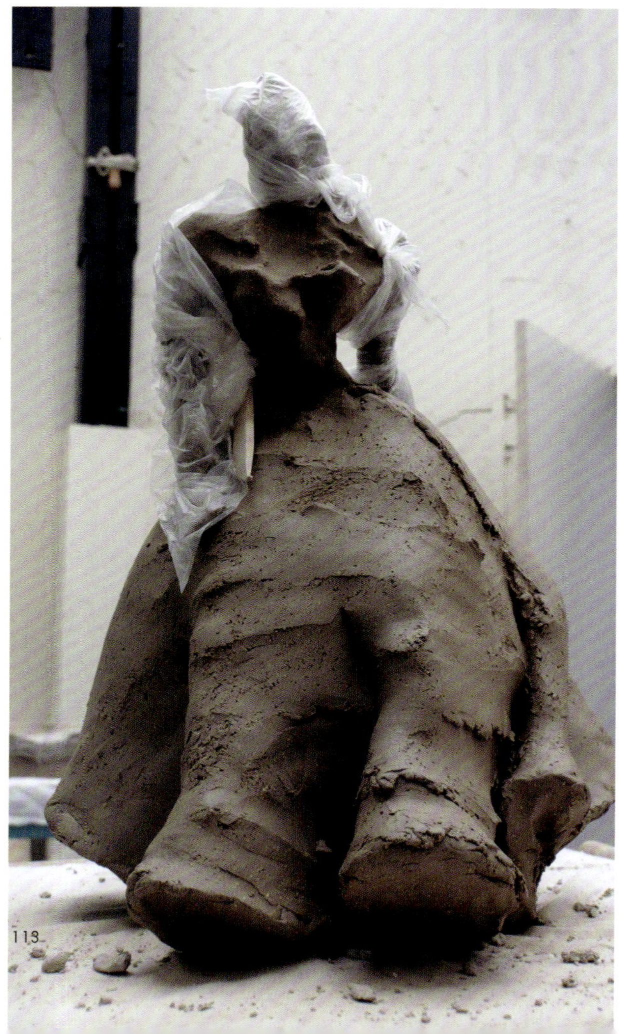

113

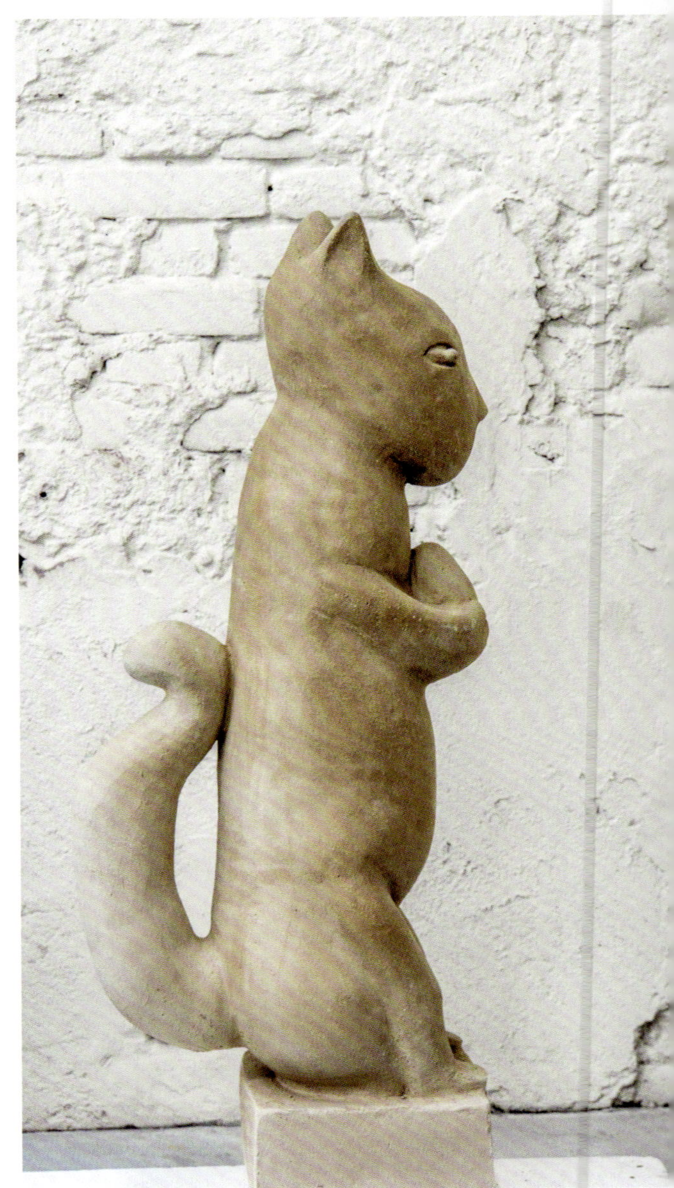

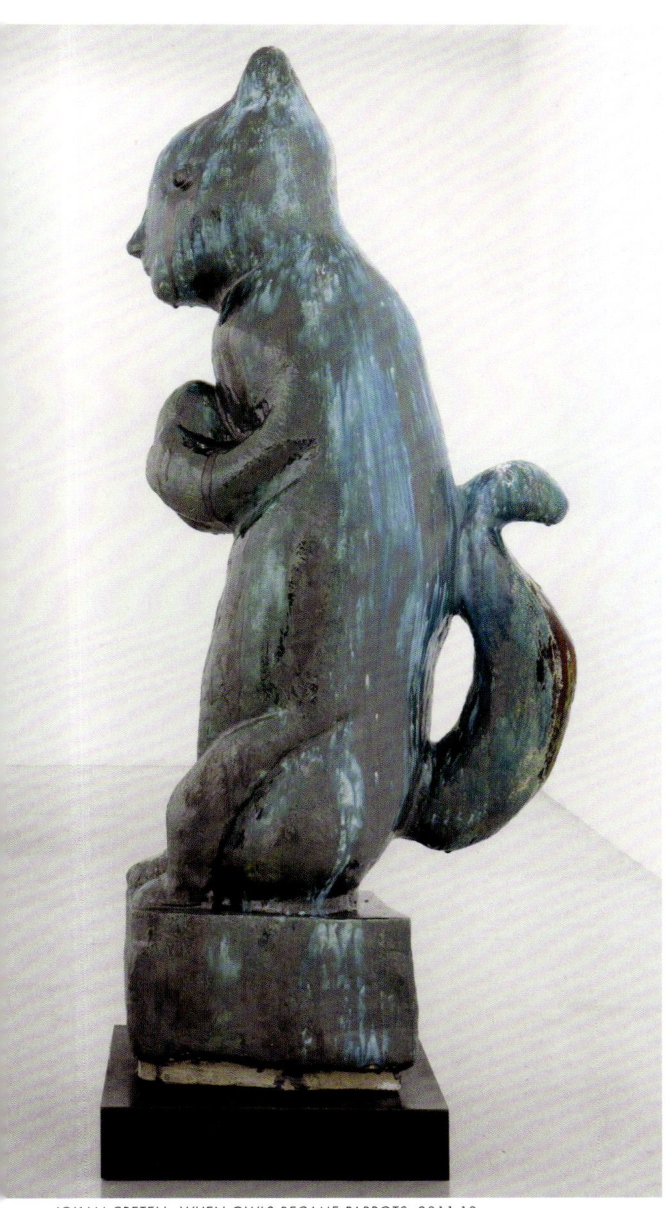

JOHAN CRETEN, *WHEN OWLS BECAME PARROTS*, 2011-12

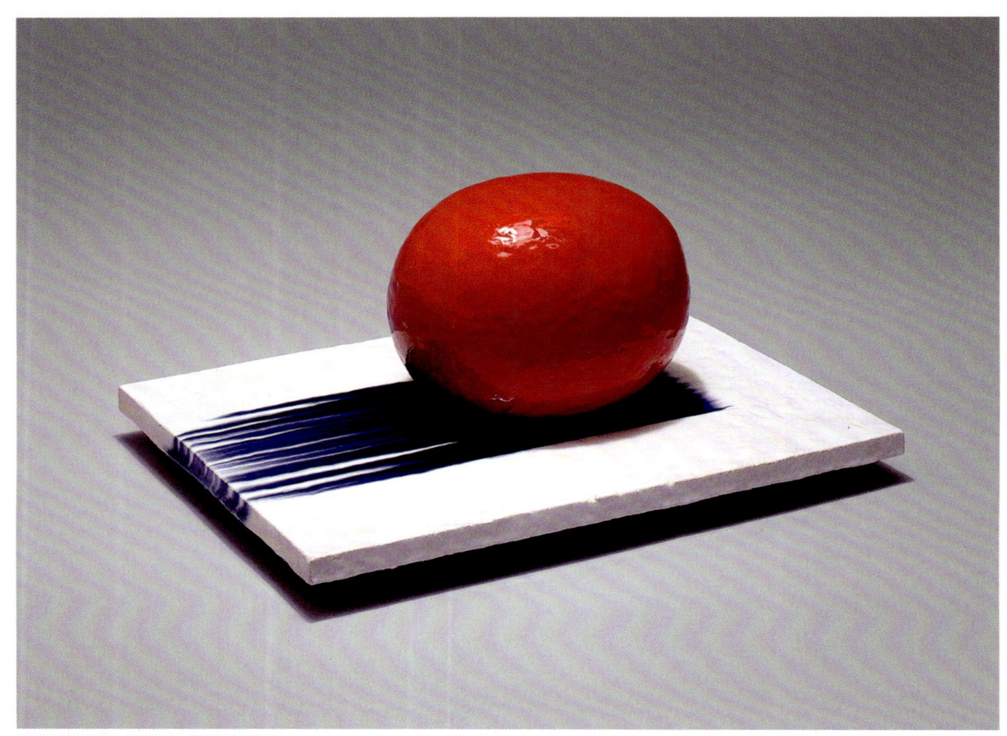

JUN KANEKO, *ITALIAN DREAM*, 1996

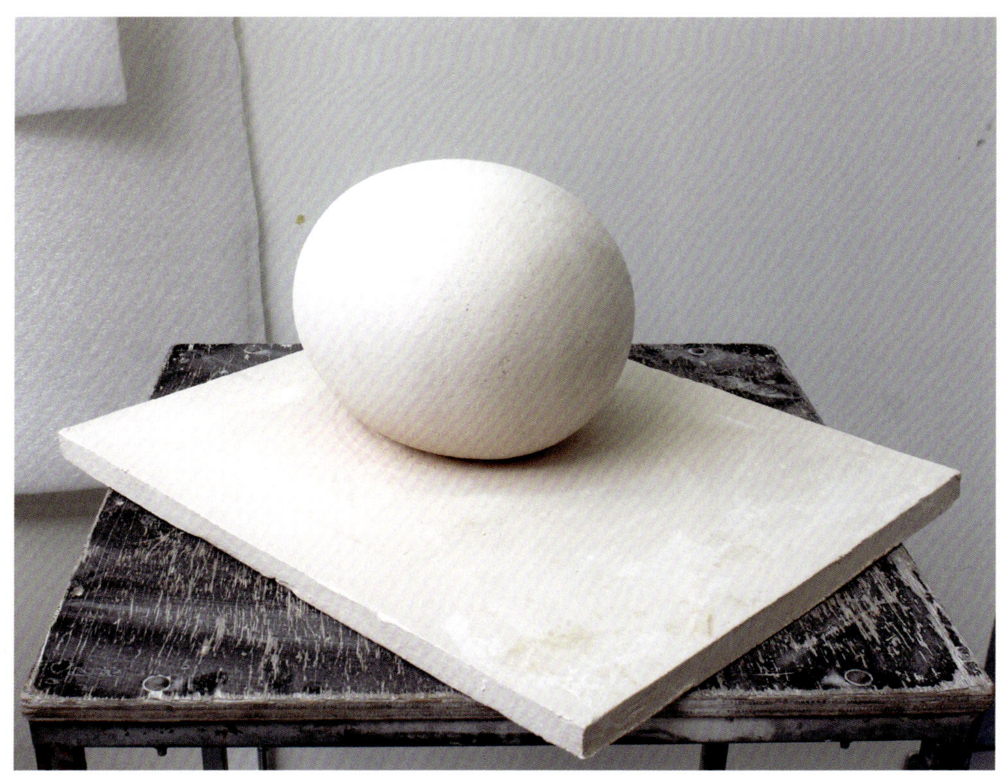

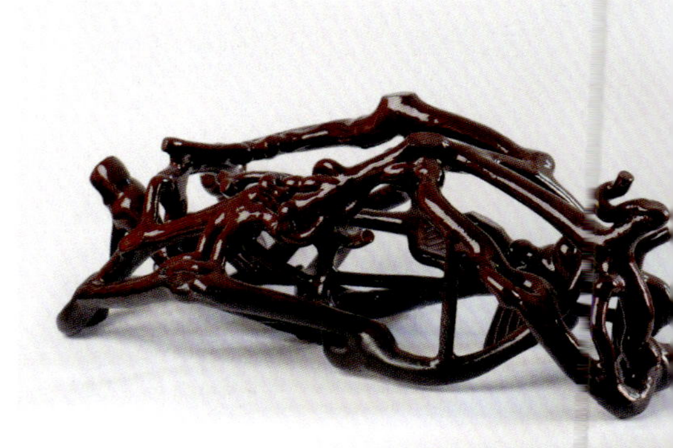

NEIL FORREST, *THICKET*, 2005

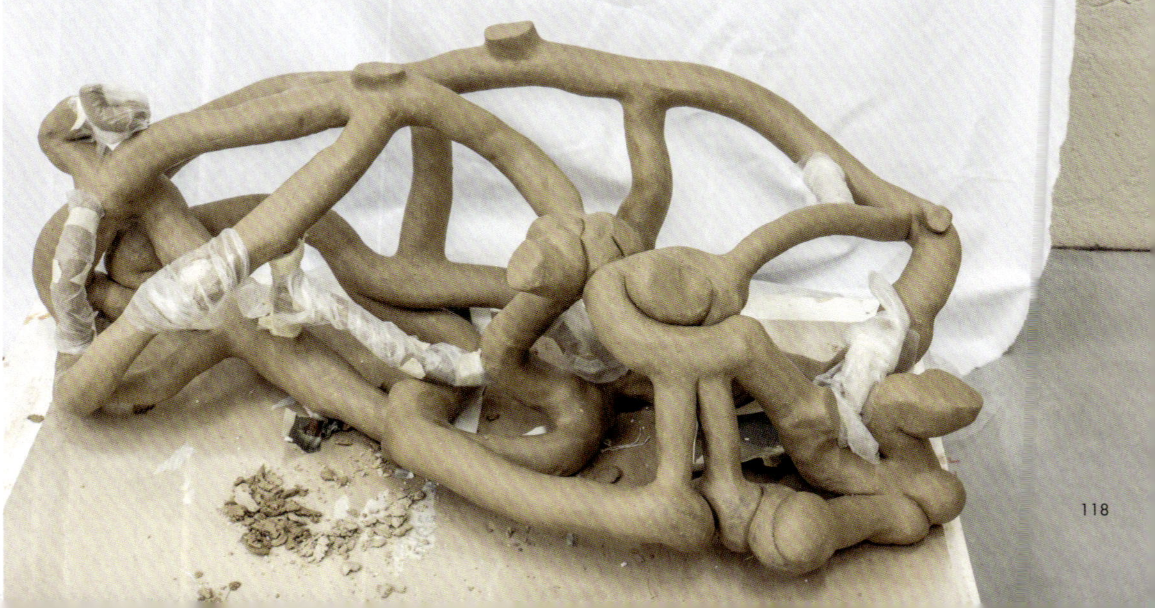

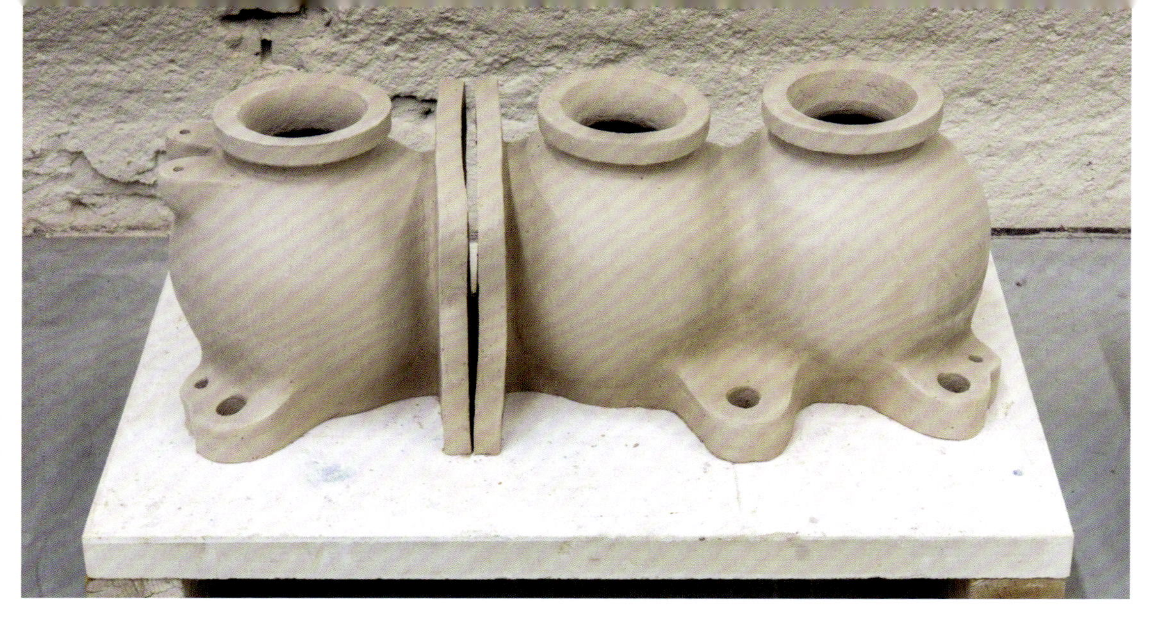

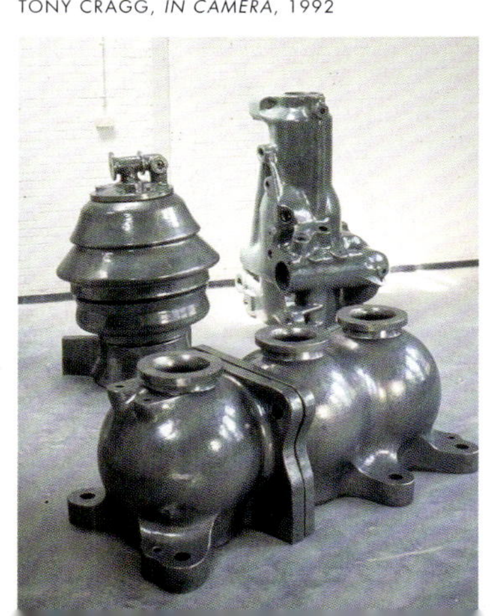

TONY CRAGG, *IN CAMERA*, 1992

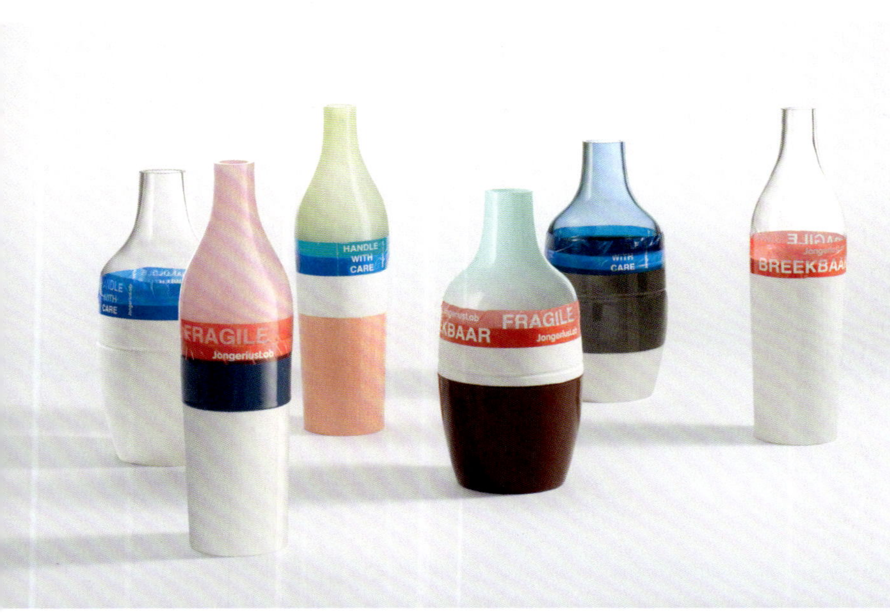

HELLA JONGERIUS, *LONG NECK AND GROOVE BOTTLES*, 2000

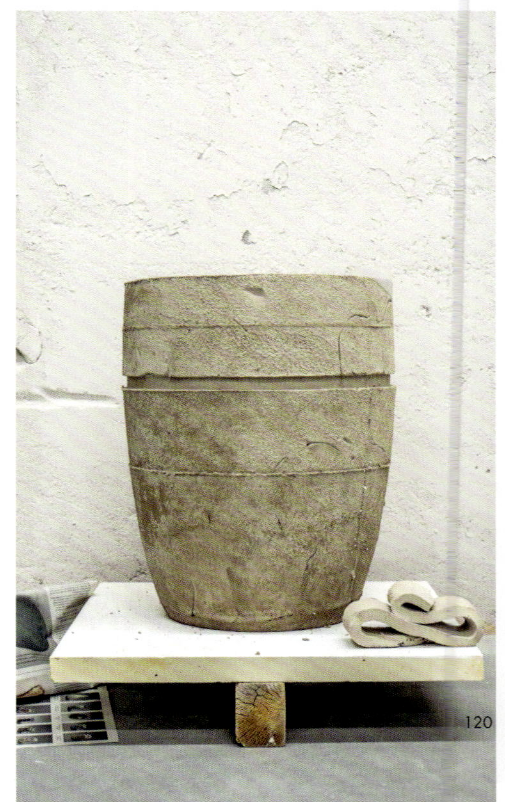

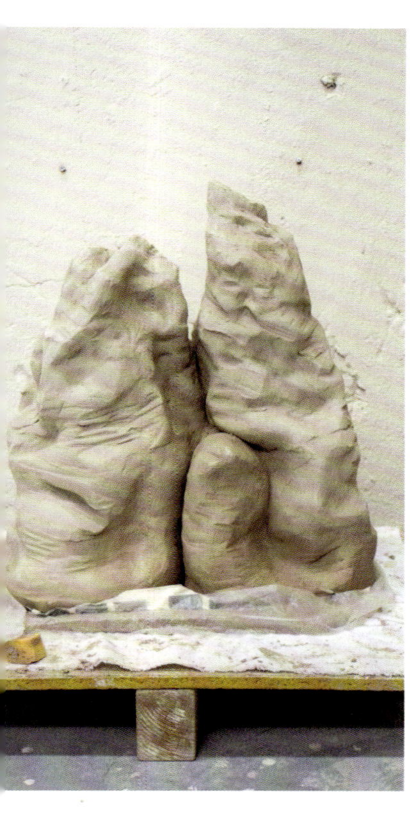

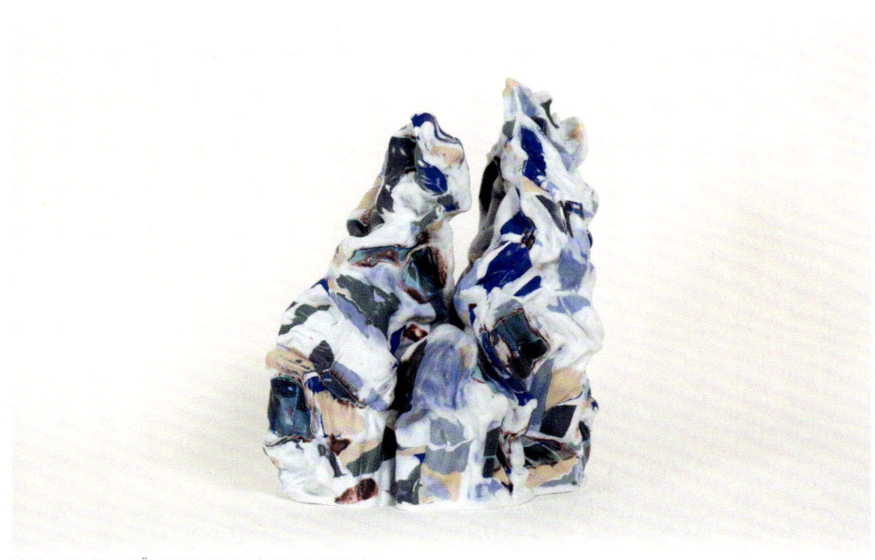

BABS HAENEN, *GÖNGSHI-THE SILK ROAD*, 2015-16

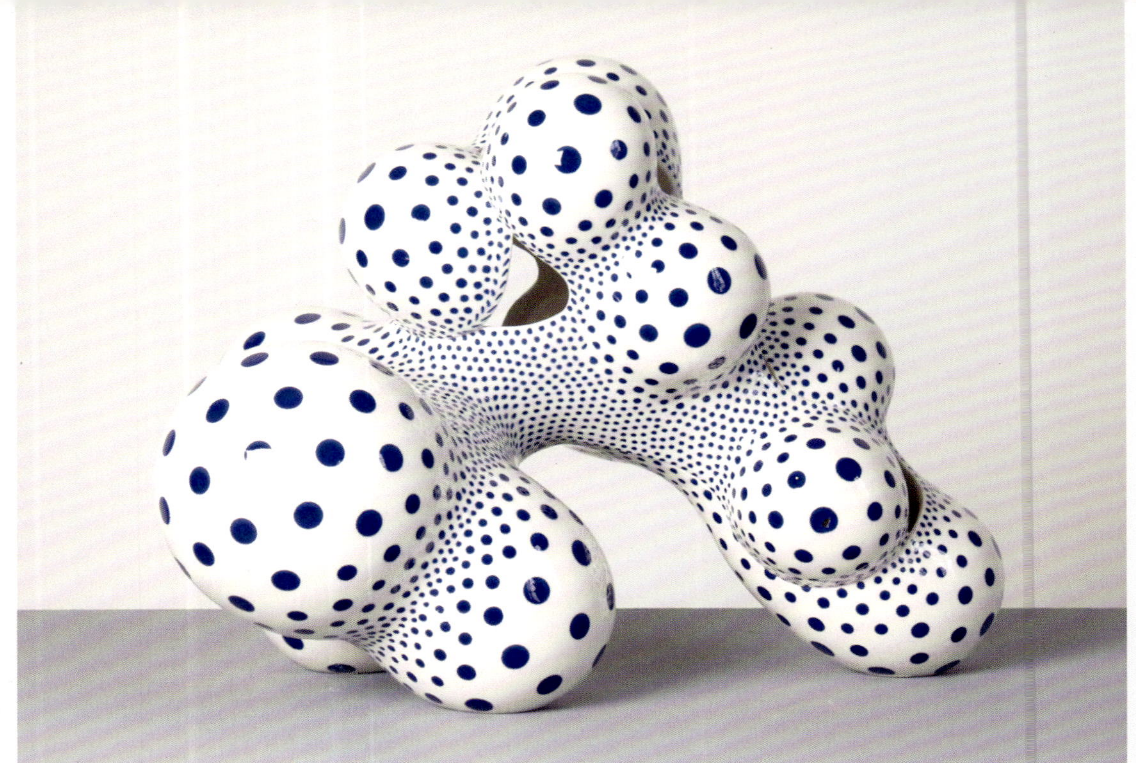

HARUMI NAKASHIMA, *A STRUGGLING FIGURE EO-1*, 2002

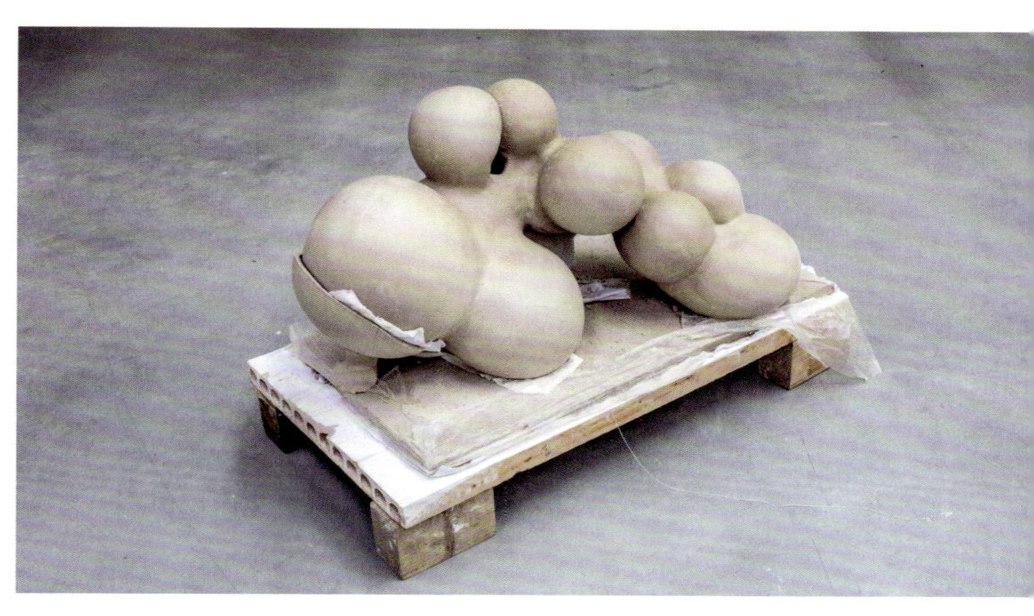

Colophon

This book was published on the occasion of the 50 years anniversary of Sundaymorning@EKWC and the forthcoming exhibition 'The Ghosts of Sunday Morning' in Design Museum Den Bosch (2 March - 19 May 2019).

Text: Glenn Adamson

Copy editing: D'Laine Camp

Design: Trapped in Suburbia

Photography: Rudi Klumpkens,

Leonie Oomen (p. 40, bottom; p.78)

Printing: UNICUM | By Gianotten, Tilburg

Paper: Magno Matt 135 gr

Publisher: Milou van Lieshout, nai010 publishers, Rotterdam

Although every effort was made to find the copyright holders for the illustrations used, it has not been possible to trace them all. Interested parties are requested to contact nai010 publishers, Korte Hoogstraat 31, 3011 GK Rotterdam, the Netherlands.

nai010 publishers is an internationally orientated publisher specialized in developing, producing and distributing books in the fields of architecture, urbanism, art and design.
www.nai010.com

Thanks to: Creative Industries Fund NL, Timo de Rijk, Fredric Baas, Marte Rodenburg, Sundaymorning@EKWC workshop team: Sander Alblas, Froukje van Baren, Rinke Joosten, Katrin Konig, Tjalling Mulder, Pierluigi Pompei, Peter Oltheten, Marianne Peijnenburg.

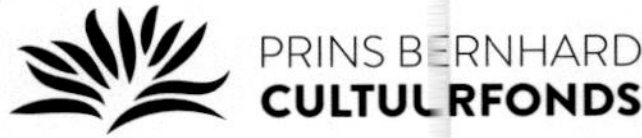

nai010 books are available internationally at selected bookstores and from the following distribution partners:
- North, Central and South America - Artbook | D.A.P., New York, USA, dap@dapinc.com
- Rest of the world - Idea Books, Amsterdam, the Netherlands, idea@ideabooks.nl

For general questions, please contact nai010 publishers directly at sales@nai010.com or visit our website www.nai010.com for further information.

Printed and bound in the Netherlands
ISBN 9789462084940
NUR 644
BISAC ART 045000 ART 006000